Black
Consciousness
In
South
Africa

SUNY Series in African Politics and Society
Henry L. Bretton and
James Turner, Editors

Black Consciousness In South Africa

The Dialectics
of Ideological Resistance
to White Supremacy

Robert
Fatton
Jr.

State University of New York Press

Published by
State University of New York Press, Albany

© 1986 State University of New York

For information, address State University of New York
Press, State University Plaza, Albany, N.Y., 12246

Library of Congress Cataloging in Publication Data

Fatton, Robert.
    Black consciousness in South Africa.

    (SUNY series in African politics and society)
    Revision of the author's thesis (Ph.D)—University of Notre Dame.
    Bibliography: p. 171
    1. Blacks—South Africa—Politics and government. 2. Blacks—South Africa—Race
identity. 3. South Africa—Politics and government—1961-1978. 4. South Africa—
Politics and government—1978-   . 5. South Africa—Social conditions—1961-   .
6. Blacks—South Africa—Social conditions. 7. South Africa—Race relations. I. Title.
II. Series.

DT763.6.F37 1986   305.8'00968   85-2855
ISBN 0-88706-127-3
ISBN 0-88706-129-X (pbk.)

10 9 8 7 6 5 4 3 2 1

CONTENTS

v

ACKNOWLEDGMENTS

This book on the Black Consciousness Movement of South Africa grew out of a doctoral dissertation prepared for the Department of Government of the University of Notre Dame. It owes a great deal to Professor Peter Walshe, the director of my thesis, whose commitment to social justice and a more humane society sharpened my interests in the politics of development and guided my attention to movements of popular resistance to oppression and racism. I am also indebted to him for choosing the South African predicament as the testing ground of my ideas and arguments. It was his stimulating graduate seminar on Southern Africa that focused my mind on this troubled and conflict-ridden region of the world. It is with the greatest gratitude and respect that I wish to acknowledge his profound influence on this book without implicating him in its shortcomings. I wish also to thank him for his friendship and continuous intellectual and moral support as well as for providing me with a source of education and inspiration.

Thanks are due as well to Dr. James Turner, Director of Africana Studies at Cornell University and Editor of the SUNY Series in African Politics and Society, who read the manuscript with care and offered many valuable suggestions.

My debt to others who contributed to the making of this book is considerable. My former teachers, Lee Roy Berry, Peter Moody, Michael Francis and Gilburt Loescher generously directed and encouraged me during my undergraduate and graduate years. An acknowledgment of gratitude is also due to Daniel Britz, Bibliographer of Africana at the Northwestern University Library for guiding me through the maze of South African documents and materials.

I wish also to thank my new colleagues at the University of Virginia and in particular Alan Cafruny for our daily and animated discussions, and Dante Germino for allowing me to teach with him a seminar on Marx and Gramsci. Indeed, this seminar strengthened my conviction in the indispensability of the Marxian tradition in the study of society and social change. It is in this tradition that I have rooted the analytical framework of this book.

A book, however, requires also the disciplined leisure of thinking and reading, of researching and writing, all of which are impossible without financial support. Accordingly, I wish to acknowledge a research grant from the Zahm Research Travel Fund of the University of Notre Dame, a generous fellowship from the Institute for the Study of World Politics, and a summer research grant from the University of Virginia. I wish also to acknowledge the Carter G. Woodson Institute and in particular Mary Rose for giving me access to their typing facilities.

But it is to my wife Kathie, that I owe the deepest thanks for her loving support, encouragement, and patience during this undertaking. To my daughter, Vanessa, who was born during the preparation of this work my loving apologies for not "having the time" to be a better father. Finally I dedicate this book to my parents with love, gratitude and respect for all that they have given me.

ROBERT FATTON, JR.
Charlottesville, Virginia,
January 17, 1985

ABBREVIATIONS

ANC	African National Congress
AZAPO	Azanian People's Organization
BAWU	Black Allied Workers' Union
BCM	Black Consciousness Movement
BCP	Black People Community Programs
BPC	Black People's Convention
BWP	Black Workers' Project
COD	Congress of Democrat
CPSA	Communist Party of South Africa
CYL	Congress Youth League
NF	National Forum
NUSAS	National Union of South African Students
PAC	Pan Africanist Congress
SACPO	South African Colored Peoples Organization
SACTU	South African Congress of Trade Unions
SADF	South African Defense Forces
SAIC	South African Indian Congress
SASM	South African Students' Movement
SASO	South African Students' Organization
SRC	Students' Representative Council
SSRC	Soweto Students' Representative Council
UCM	University Christian Movement
UDF	United Democratic Front

Chapter I

Black Consciousness from a Historical Perspective

The history of South Africa can be viewed as the history of black resistance to white conquest and white domination. This resistance has taken many forms which naturally underwent profound modifications in the years following the arrival of the first colonists led by Jan Van Riebeeck in 1652. Each form of resistance represented a specific reaction and attempted solution to the political, material, and organizational problems generated by white hegemony; each expressed simultaneously continuity and rupture with the practices of the past.

The forms of African resistance were determined by changes in African needs and consciousness, and by the structural transformations in the economic and political systems. In turn, these changes and structural transformations imposed serious limitations on the effectiveness of African resistance since they were seldom initiated or controlled by Africans. Moreover, for more

1

than half of the twentieth century, the cultural hegemony of white liberal values and white bourgeois lifestyles made it difficult for several generations of African nationalists to radically oppose a system to which they owed many loyalties and allegiances.[1]

Furthermore, the tangible and painful memories of pre-twentieth century defeats had a chilling effect on the vigor of African resistance. Nonetheless, they preserved the dignity of future generations of Africans.[2] The forms of resistance were therefore bound by the historical and social context in which they originated and matured. They were and still are determined by the means of livelihood and the mode of production; by the elements of continuity linking them to one another; by the iconoclastic departures differentiating them from one another; by the connections between ideological discourses and class interests as well as by the intellectual contributions of exogenous forces.

All of these forms of resistance, however, had as their common denominator the continuous history of African opposition to white supremacy and exploitation. Thus, despite social change and economic transformations, they represented a reaction to the basic condition of African oppression, and as such they were imbued with an ongoing sense of outrage and injustice. From this perspective, the forms of African resistance share a common ground which transcends their differences and particularisms.

The objective of this book is to analyze the ideology of these forms of resistance to white supremacy and specifically to trace the development and radicalization of the Black Consciousness Movement (BCM) of South Africa, which emerged during the late 1960's with the formation of the South African Student's Organization (SASO) and crystalized in the Black People's Convention (BPC). The whole movement was eventually banned by the white minority regime in 1977 in the aftermath of the Soweto Rebellions of 1976. Nonetheless, several organizations rooted in the tradition of Black Consciousness such as the Azanian People's Organization (AZAPO) and the National Forum (NF) crystalized in the late 1970's and early 1980's to fill the vacuum created by the bannings.

Any consideration of Black Consciousness must begin, however, with an analysis of the different strands of African nationalism which developed in the first sixty years of the twentieth century and gave rise to the African National Congress (ANC) and the Pan Africanist Congress (PAC). Since their inception, these two movements have embodied the two fundamental approaches which characterize African nationalism. Created on January 8, 1912, the ANC has always invoked "multiracialism" in its opposition to white supremacy,[3] while the PAC, founded in 1959 as a reaction to this very multiracialism, embraced "Africanism"[4] as its means of overcoming the apartheid regime.

The concept of multiracialism implies a strategy bent on uniting all anti-racist forces—irrespective of their colors—in a common front and in a common fight against white supremacy. This strategy does not deny, however, the unique historical experience of African peoples as the downtrodden of the earth, but it seeks to transcend the consciousness of race and of being black into an all encompassing movement of protest. In other words, the assertion and affirmation of one's Africanness does not preclude interracial alliances and collaboration in the revolt against racialist and segregationist social structures.

It is true that in its early formulation, multiracialism was marked by the ascendancy of the missionary–liberalism of a westernized, African petty bourgeoisie which sought to gain the respect of white authorities rather than the loyalty of the African masses.[5] It is also true that multiracialism could and indeed did degenerate into a white paternalism and relegated Africans to secondary roles. Finally, it is also true that multiracialism downgraded and ultimately contributed to the denigration of any sense of pride in an African identity and decidedly promoted a distinctly European heritage and set of traditions. Yet, multiracialism in its vision of a broadly based movement transcending race and color imparted to African nationalism a humane and potentially radical understanding of the African predicament.

Indeed, the concept of multiracialism contained an embryonic understanding of class and revolution. For if interracial alliances indicated that some whites had departed from and rejected the patterns of white racism to join in the struggle for a more egalitarian society, they could conversely point to the fact that exploitation was not necessarily anchored in a particular race and that the coming to power of a black government would not necessarily lead to an egalitarian, and good society. Thus, multiracialism can properly be appreciated as implanting in the vast field of African nationalism the seeds of a radical and indeed socialist alternative.

In other words, the nonexclusive character of multiracialism represents a minor term of a dialectical process whereby the simultaneous consciousness of race and the acceptance of interracial unity are the element negating white supremacy. It is an insufficient element, however, as the full unfolding of the dialectics requires the creation of a society without races and without classes. Accordingly, multiracialism is a transitory means to an ultimate end; it is the vehicle of the potential transformation of African nationalism into genuine socialism.[6]

In contradistinction to the multiracialism of the ANC, the PAC, which originated in the ANC's Congress Youth League[7] of the 1940's, preached the virtues of an undiluted African nationalism. This undiluted nationalism was based on the conviction that Africans had to reject collaboration as well as alliances with both whites and the other South African ethnic groups. Only such exclusively African movements, argued the PAC, could liberate Africans from their cultural inferiority, material deprivation, and social humiliation.[8] Africans, in the PAC's Africanist view, were to no longer understand their position through European lenses, nor were they to borrow the language and practices of white liberals in their quest for liberation; rather, they were to formulate their own vision of the world and select the ways to transform it. Africans had to free themselves from their cultural and economic dependence; they had to become independent and autonomous agents.

Liberation presupposed a rupture with the values and ways of life of the colonizer, and an adaptation of the African heritage to the conditions of the modern world. The African condition under apartheid, Africanists argued, generated not just defeatism and poverty but also moral degradation and self-hatred. Africans developed such an acute sense of inferiority that their color had become a symbol of sin, their history an episode of savage barbarism, and their culture a badge of backwardness and ignorance. In this pathetic context, Africans had espoused the norms and values of the colonizer; they had come to believe that being civilized meant to whiten their souls and reject their blackness. Anton Lembede, the first president of the Congress Youth League (CYL) and the father of Africanism, expressed the sentiment as follows:

> Moral and spiritual degeneration manifests itself in such abnormal and pathological phenomena as loss of self confidence, inferiority complex, a feeling of frustration, the worship and idolisation of white man, foreign leaders and ideologies. All these are symptoms of a pathological state of mind.[9]

The cure for this loss of African identity was the development of nationalism. But it was nationalism with a difference: Africans were called to fulfill their divine destiny by developing their deepest will with the "fanaticism and bigotry of religion."[10] Nationalism was to guarantee higher intentions, the blessing of a better world and the greatest advance of the African mind. Hence, nationalism was the essential link in the African chain of liberation. Without it, Africans were doomed to failure and nothingness; they would yearn for Europeanization; they would admire the white world and despise their own. Africanism embodied then the total rejection of European leadership and black inferiority. It was the ideological expression of the birth of African self-assertion and defiance.

The development of an assertive African nationalism constituted, therefore, the central aim of the Africanists. To assure such development, Africanists proposed a policy of independence, in which Africans had to regroup as Africans and reject cooperation with representatives of other races. Such attitudes indicated not racism, but rather a desire to root out any sense of African inferiority through the creation of a higher degree of cohesion and self-confidence. To cooperate with other races at this juncture of history was to commit suicide. Africans would be manipulated by these other races as they lacked assurance in their goals and organizational strength as a group. Moreover, Africans, Africanists argued, were different; they had a special heritage which could neither be understood nor truly appreciated by other people—particularly the European colonizers.[11]

The new African spirit welded individual wills into an organic whole and it expressed the corporate nature of communal life. Such spirit was embedded in the conviction that historical forces were inevitably leading to self-realization, freedom, and harmony; the individual was absorbed into the organic whole and his will became inseparable from the will of the collectivity. Not surprisingly, Africanists were ideologically opposed to European bourgeois individualism. Such individualism, Africanists contended, bred continual and deadly conflicts for Africans who were striving for ultimate unity and collective order.[12] The fragmentation and alienation of social life induced by the racial capitalism of South Africa represented in the eyes of Africanists an evil of major proportion that denied the realization of the true African personality.

The Africanist rejection of bourgeois values did not imply, however, acceptance of Marxian communism.[13] In fact, for Africanists who tended to explain and understand the predicament of Africans under apartheid in terms of race and racism, the Marxian emphasis on class as the root cause of social injustice and rebellion was quite unconvincing and unappealing. The differences between Africanism and Marxism reflected two opposing world-views: one emphasized a race-conscious nationalism as a creed capable of rousing Africans to political awareness and action; the other stressed the class struggle both within and without racial boundaries as a means of seeing the national struggle as an interim stage in the process of moving on to a social revolution. This opposition does not mean, however, that the two positions were totally irreconcilable. Indeed, most Africanists were prepared to envisage some form of socialism, but this vision paled before the primacy of an assertive nationalism. In the words of Lembede: "The achievement of national liberation will . . . usher in a new era, the era of African socialism. Our immediate task, however, is not socialism, but national liberation."[14]

This belief in the primacy of nationalism over socialism also animated the multiracialists of the ANC. Such a belief was not merely the reflection of simple ideological preferences; it was also a symptom of deeper structural realities. The advocates of both Africanism and multiracialism formed what was essentially a petty bourgeoisie; they were the products of missionary education and they poorly represented the concerns of the African peasantry and proletariat.[15] Their inadequacy, however, stemmed not only from an ingrained timidity and moderation, but above all from their objective position in a class structure which, however radically determined, separates Africans themselves into conflicting social strata.[16]

This separation was a massive chasm in the early period of the twentieth century. During that era the African petty bourgeoisie committed to white bourgeois values did not experience systemic exploitation as misery and hunger, but as a racial obstacle to its move into a colorless bourgeoisie. It was this desire to climb up into the place of the white bourgeoisie which explains the conservatism and even reactionary character of the African petty bourgeoisie. Bluntly stated, while the "congeries of interests, social experiences, traditions, and value systems"[17] of the black petty bourgeoisie strengthened its ties and connections to the white capitalist class, they weakened its attachment to the peasant and proletarian African world. It did not matter that the petty bourgeoisie, proletariat and peasantry were of the same race; the conflict of class interests cut across color lines and exercised a profound influence on the historical development of African nationalism. Hence it is misleading to explain the moderation of black opposition in the early period of the twentieth century solely in terms of "naiveté" and "unrealism."[18] Such moderation existed because an African petty bourgeoisie monopolized the political leadership of black resistance and envisaged its future as one of upward mobility into the spheres of white bourgeois privileges.

In this early period of the twentieth century, the majority of African leaders envisaged the liberation of their people in terms of their progressive integration into the "democratic" process of white society. For such leaders, liberation meant gradual entry into the established structures of the white polity; by no means did it imply a radical and revolutionary departure from the norms and practices of the day. Not surprisingly, this leadership considered "[a] 'civilisation test', that is a 'reasonable measure of education and material contribution to the welfare of the country' . . . equitable as the basis for a qualified franchise."[19] The implication is plain: those Africans who possessed neither capital nor education were incapable of a fully rational life; they lacked the attributes of civilized men.

Thus, the African petty bourgeois leadership, as regards its paternalism towards the masses and its apprehension at radicalizing them, revealed its class interests rather than a mere misconception of the power structure. It is true that these petty bourgeois leaders "persisted in believing against all the evidence that liberation would come to them through reasoned argument, appeals to Christain ethics, and moderate, constitutional protest."[20] However, these beliefs reflected not so much their timidity or want of confidence, but rather the class parameters within which they operated. Consciously or unconsciously, the African petty bourgeoisie rationalized its conservative class interests and Victorian worldview by presenting itself as the rising class, the bearer and defender of African history.

Thus, long sustained by the colonial educational system which pushed its relatively few African graduates into the westernized petty bourgeoisie, the ideology of promotion and climbing-up into the bourgeoisie retarded the process of mass organization and thwarted the emergence of African ideological militancy. It was only when disillusionment under the impact of persisting racial discrimination and repression crushed this ideology of promotion that the African petty bourgeoisie—and then only a fraction of it—felt compelled to adopt the idiom and the practice of revolution, an ideological transformation which crystalized only in the late 1950's.

During the late 1940's and 1950's, the African political leadership was forced to radicalize as a result of the increasing intransigence of white power and the mounting wave of racist and segregationist legislation enacted by the newly elected Afrikaner Nationalist Party in 1948.[21] In addition, the militant activities of CYL during the 1940's had also contributed to the collapse of the conservative old guard which had hitherto guided the ANC.[22] This in turn further opened up the prospect for the increasing radicalization of African resistance, even if it brought to the fore the thorny problem of deciding what kind of ideology and political processes would replace the somewhat amorphous attitudes and tactics of earlier struggles. In this context, it is crucial to analyze briefly the major political undertakings of the ANC during the 1950's, as these precipitated the official scission of African nationalism into the multiracialist ANC and the Africanist PAC.

The ideals which finally triumphed in the 1950's were those championed by CYL and embodied in the Program of Action.[23] The acceptance of this program was precipitated by the alarm and panic caused by the 1948 victory of Malan's Afrikaner Nationalist Party and the subsequent recognition that apartheid had to be fought with increasing determination. Such determination characterized the Program of Action which called for extra-constitutional mass action through the mobilization of the African population. However, if a new militancy was asserted, political goals and ideological directions within the broader movement of the ANC remained confused and sketchy. As with the earlier Africans' Claims[24] the Program of Action committed the ANC to pursue "national freedom from white domination," "political independence," and "self-determination"; but what was meant by these goals was never precisely explained.[25]

The Program of Action nevertheless reflected a radicalism which was absent from Africans' Claims in that it insisted on extra-legal actions and abandoned the hope of white benevolence. On the other hand, this radicalism had yet to produce a serious economic analysis. What Professor Walshe has written about CYL's statements is equally applicable to the Program of Action which the ANC had come to accept under the pressure of the youth:

> Little detailed thinking . . . was apparent at the level of a future South Africa economic policy. . . . The most widespread inclination appears to have been for some limited nationalisation of industry

and the establishment of a welfare state, much on the lines of the British Labour Party's policy.[26]

While the hardening of racism helped to arouse a new militancy, this new consciousness was not as yet focused on the necessity of radically altering the material basis of society. The African petty bourgeois leadership had no doubt undergone a profound transformation in terms of its understanding of white politics but its economic vision was still clouded by the myth of equal opportunity, as if such a formula would automatically redress disparities of wealth and power. Thus, at this juncture of African history,

> . . . men responded to . . . the great emotive themes set going by the war: the spectacle of powerful non-white nationalism in the shape of Japan or the militant campaigns of the Indian National Congress; the anti-Nazi propaganda of the Allies that was also, and unavoidably as the democratizing pressures of the war continued, an anti-racist propaganda; and, perhaps most of all, the stirring promise of the Atlantic Charter drawn up in August 1941 by Roosevelt and Churchill. 'Freedom nothing but freedom' was the call that seized the imagination alike of the many and the few. Let freedom come, and everything would change.[27]

Skeptics who viewed "freedom" without profound economic transformation as an incomplete and insufficient demand, fell under suspicion and condemnation. Those who dared to question the primacy of the concept of color and embraced the concept of class were judged to be dangerous dogmatists spreading an alien ideology antipathetic to the emerging nationalist gospel. This tension, the deepening hostility between Africanists and Marxists and the increasing influence of the Communist Party of South Africa (CPSA)[28] on the liberation movement, became most apparent during the 1940's when CYL made repeated attempts to expel communists from the ANC.

Within the Africanist movement itself, however, there was a small circle, headed by Willie Nkomo and Joe Matthews, which was predisposed to adopt some Marxist categories and terms. In this context, and with the rather desperate need for cooperation that a growing opposition to apartheid entailed, ideological tensions and antipathies between Africanist and Marxists were curbed.

A new ideological trend was thus introduced by the closer interaction between Africanists and Marxists. Although eclectic and still tentative, such interaction was in part the result of African disillusionment with liberal niceties and Christian incantations. By 1951 this disillusion was clear. In his presidential address to CYL, Joe Matthews argued that:

> . . . the possibility of a liberal capitalist democracy in South Africa is exactly nil. The racialist propaganda amongst the whites and their desire to maintain what they imagine to be a profitable situation makes it utterly unthinkable that there can be a political alignment that favours a liberal white group. In any case the political immorality, cowardice and vacillation of the so-called progressives amongst the whites render them utterly useless as a force against fascism.[29]

Matthews also argued that the quest for liberation in South Africa was an integral part of the larger colonial struggle against European imperialism, an imperialism supported by the "indirect enemy," America. This struggle against imperialism was also a struggle against "Capitalism [which had] developed to monopolism and [was] now reaching the final stage of monopoly capital gone mad, namely fascism."[30] Victory in this struggle would be secured by the "labour power of the African people [which could be] unleashed at short notice by determined leadership."[31]

Thus, by the late 1940's the ANC had been rejuvenated, earlier beliefs in liberalism and constitutionalism had been seriously eroded, and a new enthusiasm for mass action and extra-legal protests was present. While this militantism had its roots in CYL, it was also induced by the activism and yet prudent legalism of Xuma's presidency. Recognizing the need for an organizationally strong and politically more militant movement, Xuma called for a mass membership drive encompassing Africans of all social strata—chiefs and peasants, workers and petty bourgeois, men and women. Indeed, "every African" was to participate in the revitalization of Congress.[32] However, this revitalization was only partially successful:

> In the course of the 1940's, Congress had been firmly re-established as the national organisation of the African people . . . formal membership rose to about 5,000 with an unknown number of supporters hanging loose or in affiliated organisations. The ANC was seen by hundreds of thousands of Africans to voice their aspirations, even if they watched their political vanguard from outside the formal branch, provincial and national structure. Congress had in fact been brought very close to the fullest extent of its organisational potential given the limitations within which it functioned.[33]

The causes of these limitations were not only financial and logistical; they were also due to increasing police surveillance and to the persistent fear of uncompromising confrontation with white authorities. Yet, by the end of the 1940's Congress was forced to radicalize further if it was to avoid a return to stagnation and decay. In the industrialized context of modern South African capitalism, Congress' hopes for survival and relevance depended on its ability to gain the massive support of urban Africans. The methods and ideology of earlier struggles would not do. Radicalism was becoming a practical necessity. And it was on this issue of further radicalization that Xuma's presidency came to end. His fears of massive state reprisals led him to reject the more assertive and militant policies adopted by Congress under the pressures of CYL.

However, these policies were not simply the result of CYL's pressures; the presence of groups prepared to call for mass resistance, strikes and civil disobedience, produced also, by way of reaction, the ANC's "pull" to the left. Hence, the radicalization of African ideology became inevitable, once more militant movements like the African Democratic Party, the Non-European Movement, and the All African Convention[34] challenged both the conservatism of the ANC and its political supremacy.

The new militancy of the ANC was also bolstered by the experience of the massive African mine workers' strike of 1946.[35] This strike seemed to prove unequivocally the readiness of the masses for vigorous political action and the obsolescence of constitutionalism and legalism. The brutal breaking of the strike by white authorities marked the beginnings of the communist witch hunt which culminated in the Suppression of Communism Act of 1950.[36] Such use of violence and tampering with civil liberties further eroded any residual African faith in white liberalism. The ANC began to realize that it had to channel the energies and resources of the masses if they were not to be wasted in desperate and ill-conceived revolts. These new radical convictions ushered in the Defiance Campaign of 1952.

Induced by the common effort of the ANC and the South African Indian Congress (SAIC), the Defiance Campaign was intended "to declare war"[37] on the constitutional structures of apartheid; but as the new ANC leader Dr. Moroka stressed in his presidential address: ". . . we ask for nothing that is revolutionary."[38] What was demanded was the repeal of all oppressive and racist laws and the immediate realization of "full democratic rights" for all South Africans irrespective of their color. While Dr. Moroka, who was essentially a compromise candidate for the presidency—a weak and outdated figurehead— conceived the Defiance Campaign as a massive appeal to whites for reconsidering their attitudes, the most widespread inclination appears to have been a popular condemnation of the "white man's laws" and a passionate call for the unity of the oppressed in their common struggle for justice.[39] The goal was no longer to convert whites by a change of heart, but rather to force them by demonstration of strength to a more conciliatory stance.

The acceptance of non violence as a form of resistance did not necessarily indicate a belief in Ghandi's ethic of Satyagraha.[40] Rather it was a deliberate and pragmatic choice, as the Report of the Joint Planning Council of the ANC and the SAIC recognized:

> With regard to the form of struggle best suited to our conditions we have been constrained to bear in mind the political and economic set-up of our country, the relationship of the rural to the urban population, the development of the trade union movement with particular reference to the disabilities and state of organization of the non-white workers, the economic status of the various sections

of the non-white people and the level of organization of the National Liberatory movements. We are therefore of the opinion that in these given historical conditions the forms of struggle for obtaining the repeal of unjust laws which should be considered are: (a) defiance of unjust laws and (b) industrial action.[41]

Although the Joint Council claimed the primacy of industrial action, it was opposed to its immediate use. The Council asserted that "industrial action is second to none, the best and most important weapon in the struggle of the people for the repeal of the unjust laws and that it is inevitable that this method of struggle has to be undertaken, at one time or another during the course of the struggle."[42] However, industrial action was to be "resorted to at a later stage in the struggle."[43]

This analysis appears to have been rooted in the conviction that the black workers' organization and consciousness were as yet too weak and uncertain for disciplined and planned action. To this must be added the continuing divisions and confusion on economic policies that forced either silence on particular issues or postponement of certain forms of resistance.[44] Hence, the choice of civil disobedience over industrial action in the planning of the Defiance Campaign stemmed from the supposed immaturity of the black proletariat and the debate on whether class or color best explained the conflict between whites and blacks.

Be that as it may, the Defiance Campaign was a clear sign of growing ideological radicalization and organizational sophistication. Planned as an escalating and sustained drive toward mass action, it called for three stages of challenge and protest: In the first, a small number of selected volunteers were to break certain racist laws in the major urban centers; in the second, the scope of action as well as the number of volunteers would be increased; in the third, the struggle would "broaden out on a country-wide scale and assume a general mass character."[45]

While it would be an exaggeration to claim that the campaign achieved its projected "mass character," it marked the first carefully planned struggle of the oppressed. It transcended tribal and racial ties and fired Africans with a sense of hope and potential power; it proved that the masses were ready to sacrifice and risk their lives for the sake of future generations. The campaign also attracted international attention to the plight of the black peoples of South Africa. However, it failed to repeal the unjust laws and "at no time did [it] shake—though it did anger—the government . . . [nor did it] ever [look] like producing anything remotely ressembling a truly revolutionary situation."[46]

Nevertheless, the government interpreted the Defiance Campaign as a revolutionary movement bent on overthrowing the structures of white supremacy and adopted harsh repressive measures—the passage in 1953 of the Public Safety Act[47] and the Criminal Laws Amendment Act.[48] So, while the Defiance Campaign boosted the Africans' morale and confidence, it failed to eradicate the unjust laws and offered new opportunities for greater repression to an already tyrannical government. The Campaign and subsequent trend toward passive resistance during the 1950's exposed the inadequacies and even futility of nonviolent and open methods of resistance in conditions of overwhelming police hostility. As the weight of repression increased and eventually both the ANC and PAC were banned after the Sharpeville massacre in 1960, the old commitment to aboveground and non-violent strategies was eroded. African leaders finally realized that the post-defiance era was "vastly different" and that the "masses had to be prepared and made ready for new forms of political struggle."[49]

However, trying to walk a tightrope between its radical and moderate wings of a broad movement, the ANC had refrained from commitment to revolutionary confrontation and in the late 1950's, had reemphasized the priority of building a centralized and disciplined mass movement. By 1954 such a movement was to be patterned according to the directives of the M-Plan which called for a hierarchical, cell-based organization of highly dedicated members. The M-Plan was named after its principal architect, Nelson Mandela who recognized that it was "no longer possible to wage our struggle mainly on the old methods of public meetings and printed circulars."[50]

The conviction spread that verging on illegality and pitted against the resources of a powerful state, the ANC had to centralize its structure and method of operation if it were to resist repression and remain effective under conditions of secrecy. In its Report of 1954, the National Executive Committee analyzed the situation as follows:

> . . . it is quite clear that Congress cannot survive unless it changes its present organisational structure . . . [The white] Nationalists are determined and mean to deprive us of and deny us the elementary human rights of freedom of speech, freedom of assembly, freedom of organisation and freedom of movement. . . . Congress must be placed on an entirely new organisational footing. . . . The organisation should be highly centralised on the national and provincial planes, but highly decentralised on the branch and membership levels. It must be re-organised along the lines laid down in the "M" Plan.[51]

However, the M-Plan was never implemented, not just because of internal "dissension, stagnation and suspicion," but also because of a deep-seated aversion to revolutionary and conspiratorial practices. The ANC had clearly recognized that non-violent strategies were failing, but its long tradition of open and peaceful political protest continued to produce a reluctance to contemplate revolutionary confrontations.

This reluctance can be clearly seen in the three resistance campaigns of 1955. The Western Areas Campaign[52] triggered by the government's decision to remove Africans from their townships and deprive them of freehold rights in areas zoned for white businesses and residences only proclaimed: "We shall not move"; but it left the form of resistance undefined. Ambiguities as to whether violence was to be used contributed to popular confusion and indecision, and to a humiliating failure to prevent the removals.

The second campaign[53] was directed against the Bantu Education Act of 1953 which provided for transferring control of schools to the Department of Native Affairs, or for continuing a private educational system with diminishing state assistance. Despite widespread and popular discontent against what was perceived as a racist attempt to educate Africans for subservience, the ANC proved incapable of channeling the unrest. In the words of Professor Karis: "Of all campaigns conducted by the ANC, the campaign against Bantu education was the most poorly planned, the most confused, and, for Africans generally, the most frustrating."[54] Thus, however united Africans may have been in their opposition to a system geared to conditioning them into accepting inferior forms of labor, their leaders' vacillation on methods of protest rendered their action impotent and futile.

The third campaign was probably the most significant because of its symbolic content. It called for a non-racial Congress of the Peoples and the formulation of a Freedom Charter embodying the vision of a future South African order. Meeting at the Congress of the People in Kliptown on June 26, 1955, the ANC, the South African Indian Congress (SAIC), the South African Colored Peoples' Organization (SACPO), and the Congress of Democrat (COD), coalesced into a formal alliance.[55] The white Liberal Party was notably absent and vehemently condemned the alliance as a Marxist inspired movement bent on establishing a communist society.[56] While the alliance was influenced by the radicalism of COD and used some Marxist language, it did not espouse communism. What was envisaged was a nonracial populist society, the outlines of which were sketched out in the Freedom Charter.

The Charter, which was to become a seminal document, reasserted the longstanding objectives of equality before the law and a universal franchise. it maintained the commitment to nonracialism. "South Africa," the Charter declared, "belongs to all who live in it, black and white."[57] But more importantly, for the first time in ANC history the Charter linked the process of political emancipation to the transformation of the economic system. To the old belief in "equal opportunity" was added a pledge to redistribute wealth and resources. The material question had merged with the national question and the resulting synthesis embodied the populist ideal. The Charter was neither a revolutionary document nor a firm socialist commitment. It embodied a populism bent on equalizing life-chances: "The material wealth beneath the soil, the banks and monopoly industry shall be transferred to the ownership of the people as a whole. . . . The land (shall be re-divided) amongst those who work it. . . . A preventive health scheme shall be run by the state."[58]

Inasmuch as these populist objectives were unrealizable in South Africa without violence, it is possible to characterize them as revolutionary.[59] But that these objectives were not in themselves revolutionary, let alone Marxist, was clearly stated by Mandela:

> Whilst the Charter proclaims democratic changes of a far-reaching nature it is by no means a blueprint for a socialist state but a programme for the unification of various classes and groupings amongst the people on a democratic basis. . . . Its declaration "The People Shall Govern!" visualises the transfer of power not to any single social class but to all the people of the country be they workers, peasants, professional men or petty bourgeoisie.[60]

The goal, therefore, was not socialism but a populism based on class cooperation and class harmony. The modest proposals guaranteeing the social protection of proletarians and peasants against extremes of poverty were conceived as diffusing the class conflict rather than ushering in socialism. And acquiescence in the formal encroachment of the state in the private economy stemmed from the conviction that this would foster the growth of a strong African bourgeoisie. In Mandela's words:

> . . . the realisation of the Charter is inconceivable, in fact impossible, unless and until these monopolies are first smashed up and the national wealth of the country turned over to the people. The breaking up and democratisation of these monopolies will open up fresh fields for the *development of a prosperous Non-European bourgeois class. For the first time in the history of this country the Non-European bourgeois will have the opportunity to own in their own name and right mills and factories, and trade and private enterprise will boom and flourish as never before.*[61]

Mandela's conscious or unconscious confusion of the people's interests with those of a potential black bourgeoisie derived from his preference for black initiatives within a nonracial capitalism over a classless socialism. While Mandela was to evolve away from this position, it testified to the caution, moderation and class sensibility of the African petty bourgeois leadership. Standing between a commitment to organize the masses for political change and a fear of triggering a wave of repression that would destroy the vulnerable movement of extra constitutional protest, African leaders were caught in a trap from which their populism could not release them. They had to use mass support if their hopes of growing into a "prosperous bourgeoisie" were to materialize. But by throwing in their lot with proleterians and peasants, they risked losing control and transforming the national struggle into a social struggle. So while it was necessary to call for mass support, it was equally necessary to remain prudent and avoid violent confrontation. In this sense, the convergence between the national and the social struggle had barely begun to crystalize and accordingly, it was contradictory and weak. Thus, Basil Davidson's general contention that such a convergence occurred throughout Africa in the 1950's as a "mutual opportunism" reflects accurately the realities of black South African politics during this period.

[Indeed, in South Africa as well as throughout the continent,] the nationalists needed the masses and the masses needed the nationalists, but for purposes by no means necessarily identical. The nationalists became "aware of their chance to exploit the social question" . . . while the multitudes likewise came to see . . . that they could have a use for literate or clever spokesmen who could argue with officials and employers.[62]

Hence, such opportunist convergence of the petty bourgeois nationalists with the social interests and objectives of the masses created a populist alliance. The question was whether such a populist alliance could withstand repression and the centrifugal forces unleashed by conflicting class interests. Given the aggressive nature of white racism and its insistence on denying all opportunities of advancement to Africans in general, the petty bourgeois nationalists were forced to continue to suffer discrimination while preserving their modest material base, or to accept the impossibility of ever becoming a strong bourgeoisie and so, start thinking about socialism and revolution. However, subsequent events were to prove that such acceptance was slow to come and by no means popular, and that there was no reason to believe that the social conditions inducing it were to persist indefinitely—a theme that will be pursued in coming chapters.

Be that as it may, the Charter represented the first serious attempt to bridge the gap between the aspirations of the few and the many, and this alone justifies Mandela's claim that it was "an event of major political significance in the life of this country."[63] Yet, the adoption of the Charter put great strains on African unity as its dedication to nonracialism came under bitter Africanist denunciations. To accept the idea that South Africa belongs to all who live in it, black and white, was to reject what the Africanists perceived as the African's inalienable rights of total ownership of South Africa. To claim that blacks and whites were "equals, countrymen and brothers," as did the Charter, was to defy the grim reality of white repression and supremacy. To cooperate with other racial groups as the ANC did, was to weaken the will of the masses and to forfeit the principles of African nationalism embodied in the Program of Action. These ideological tensions, forced to the surface by the Freedom Charter, climaxed in the Africanist break-away of 1958 and the formation of the Pan Africanist Congress (PAC) in 1959.

In 1959, Robert Sobukwe, defending the Africanist break-away, sharply condemned the policies and leadershp of the ANC. The Africanists, he argued, in contradistinction to the ANC, conceived the struggle not as a class struggle, but as a national struggle. Africans, he contended, were "oppressed as a subject nation" and not as a class. In his opinion, the ANC in its alliance with other ethnic groups was pursuing cooperation with the oppressors. Cooperation, he believed, "is possible only between equals. There can be no co-operation between oppressor and oppressed, dominating and dominated."

In Sobukwe's judgment, South Africa was the exclusive property of the Africans and this required "the complete overthrow of white domination." This approach, he argued, stemmed not from an intrinsic hatred of white people, but from a hatred of oppression: ". . . once white domination has been overthrown and the white man is no longer 'white-man boss' . . . there will be no reason to hate him and he will not be hated even by the masses."[64] Within the new South Africa there would be no "minority rights, because we think in terms of individuals, not groups." What would be ushered in was the "rule of an African majority" based on "political democracy as understood in the West." Economically there would be the "most equitable distribution of wealth," and the exploitation of the many for the benefits of a few would cease. The ultimate goal was an "Africanist Socialist Democracy," that would borrow "the best from the East and the best from the West."[65]

Through Joe Matthews the ANC responded quickly to these charges and accused the PAC of being a divisive force espousing a racialistic and exclusive nationalism. The PAC was wrong in believing that minority rights could be dispensed of in a democratic, and liberated South Africa. As Matthews argued, the ethnic heterogeneity of South Africa made it necessary

> . . . to go further than merely to recognise the right of each individual citizen of the state. It becomes essential to create conditions under which those who do not belong to the numerically superior national groups are able to develop their languages, culture and customs without let or hindrance.[66]

But more important in Matthews' judgment was the PAC's denial of class oppression. While the liberation movement had to be supra-class organization and while Africans suffered also from national oppression, he declared it was imperative to recognize the centrality of the class struggle. In Matthews' words: "In a certain historical situation the class struggle may be blurred by the national struggle, but to forget it is treason to the masses of people."[67]

While this ideological warfare raged, the Nationalist government went ahead with its plans for the further implementation of apartheid. In 1957, it passed the Native Laws Amendment, and in 1959 parliament adopted the Promotion of Bantu Self Government Act and the Extension of University Education Act. Opposition to these Acts was disorganized and ended in failure. Such disorganization derived not only from ideological divisions, but also from the effects of the Treason Trial.

The trial started in December 1956, after the arrest of 156 opponents of apartheid, represented an attempt by the state to prove that the liberatory organizations were communist-inspired and bent on overthrowing the white regime by violence. As Oswald Pirow, the chief prosecutor, put it: "The essence of the crime [was] hostile intent . . . [since] the accused must have known that the course of action pursued by them would inevitably result in a violent collision with the State resulting in subversion."[68] Moreover, Pirow accused the conspirators of being "inspired by communist fanaticism, Bantu nationalism, and racial hatred in various degrees."[69] The trial concluded in 1961, having dragged on for more than four years, with a unanimous verdict of not guilty. According to Justice Rumpff, the prosecution failed to prove that the ANC was pursuing a policy of violent confrontation and this "inevitably meant a collapse of the whole case."[70] The court, however, accused the ANC and its allies of working "to replace the present form of State with a radically and fundamentally different form of State" and of envisaging "the use of illegal means." In addition, the court found that some leaders of the liberatory movement "made themselves guilty of sporadic speeches of violence which . . . amounted to an incitement to violence." Finally, in the eyes of the court the ANC manifested "a strong left-wing tendency" which was symbolized in "anti-imperialist, anti-West and pro-Soviet" positions.[71]

Be that as it may, the trial immobilized a large section of the leadership of the liberation movement, and so doing it contributed to the decline of resistance. But if the trial had eased mass protest it had the unintended effects of heightening popular frustrations and of impelling non-African dissenters to put aside past differences and to unite more closely against the government. The trial, however, had allowed the white supremacist state to strengthen its police apparatus and to further, undisturbed, its apartheid strategy.[72]

This strengthened police apparatus was to precipitate the African rupture with non-violence and usher in a new phase of history. Whatever prospects there may have been for peaceful change largely disappeared with the Sharpeville massacre of 1960 and the ensuing bannings of the PAC and ANC. As matters came to a head, the move to violence was accelerated and the situation was entirely changed. African leaders, under the weight of increasing repression, were forced to become revolutionaries.

The event leading to Sharpeville was the launching of the PAC's Anti-Pass campaign. While people were called to observe absolute nonviolence, the choice of peaceful resistance did not derive from ethical considerations, but from purely pragmatic ones. In Sobukwe's words:

> I say quite positively, without fear of contradiction, that the only people who will benefit from violence are the government and the police. Immediately violence breaks out we will be taken up with it and give vent to our pent-up emotions and feel that by throwing a stone at a Saracen or burning a particular building we are small revolutionaries engaged in revolutionary warfare. But after a few days, when we have buried our dead and made moving grave-side speeches and our emotions have settled again, the police will round up a few people and the rest will go back to the Passes, having forgotten what our goal had been initially. Incidentally, in the process we shall have alienated the masses who will feel that we have made cannon fodder of them, for no significant purpose except for spectacular newspaper headlines.[73]

Thus, if violence was rejected this was no longer because of an aversion of everything that smacked of revolutionary activity; quite the contrary, it was because Africans in Sobukwe's words were "not *Yet* ready to kill."[74] However, "If the other side so desires," he declared prophetically, "we will provide them with an opportunity to demonstrate to the world how brutal they can be. We are ready to die for our cause. . . ."[75]

So they did on March 21, 1960, under brutal police gun fire. Sixty-seven Africans were killed, the great majority shot in the back as they fled; 186 others were wounded, among those 40 women and eight children. "If police had not shot the crowd of demonstrators that gathered at Sharpeville . . . the day might have marked just one more abortive campaign in the history of African protest."[76] Instead, a new era in the history of African resistance had begun.

This new era materialized in the creation of Umkhonto we Sizwe ("Spear of the Nation") and POQO ("We Stand Alone") as the respective military wings of the ANC and PAC. Umkhonto and POQO symbolized two distinct approaches to armed liberation and two distinct ideological and political conceptions of the role of violence.

For the ANC, the adoption of sabotage as its main weapon of combat indicated indeed a new phase in the history of black resistance, but it never led to the primacy of arms over politics. Violence, the ANC argued, could not be divorced from political action and organization. This was clearly stated by the National Executive of the ANC when in April 1963 it linked itself for the first time with Umkhonto, "The military wing of our struggle":

> Our emphasis still remains mass political action. The political wing will ever remain the necessary and integral part of the fight. Political agitation is the only way of creating the atmosphere in which military action can most effectively operate. The political front gives sustenance to the military operations. The Umkhonto cannot survive in a sterile political climate.[77]

Hence, the ANC concluded that politics as an external mediating force would be necessary to raise unorganized and spontaneous violence from the level of unproductive terrorism to that of revolutionary struggle. This conception of the "primacy of politics"[78] was what distinguished Umkhonto from POQO, the military offshoot of the PAC.

POQO lacked any clear pattern of authority and organization. It was inspired neither by a well-defined ideology nor by a specific strategy of liberation. Engaged in frankly terrorist acts of killing whites, POQO[79] subscribed to Fanon's notion that the "native life can only spring up again from the rotting corpse of the settler."[80] The spontaneous outbursts of violence were allowed as if the mere practice of murdering the white enemy embodied liberation itself. Not surprisingly, POQO failed to transform the racially motivated hatred of its down-trodden migrant and unemployed supporters into a revolutionary ideology divested of racist content and informed by political and economic awareness.

POQO's goal was "Freedom by 1963"; the motto was "kill or be killed." On March 24, 1963, the PAC's acting chief, P. K. Leballo, announced in a press conference in Maseru that POQO and the PAC were one and the same movement. POQO, he added, with its army of 150,000 men divided into 1,000 cells, was actively preparing to deliver a "knock-out-blow" on white supremacy.[81] Leballo's press conference was an act of pure folly, for not only did it prove the amateurish character of a purported underground and secret organization, but, more importantly, it facilitated the intensification of state repression. On the first of April, British colonial authorities raided PAC's headquarters in Maseru and discovered a list of the names of 10,000 to 15,000 POQO members. Immediately afterwards South African police began to arrest and jail reputed PAC adherents. POQO never recovered from the consequences of Leballo's press conference.

It is nevertheless clear that during its short period of active resistance, POQO had gained widespread popular support among Africans, while successfully terrorizing the white population. Its virulent black nationalism articulated an "anti-whiteism" which could not fail to ring a respondent chord among the poor, degraded, and downtrodden African community. But the simple message embodied in racial hatred could not by itself transform South African society. It was more symptomatic of a spontaneous moral outrage at exploitation, rather than the symbol of an emerging revolutionary alternative.

Relying exclusively on violence, discarding entirely the economic and political processes, emphasizing the spontaneity of the masses and dismissing the rigor and discipline of insurrectional organization, POQO elevated terrorism to a futile position of supremacy.[82] While terrorism and its stress on anti-white violence may liberate the masses from psychic alienation and instill in them a sense of historical confidence, it fails to politicize them and offers no insight into the social and economic mechanisms of their own exploitation. Neither does it create alternative centers of popular power and new forms of political participation which are, after all, a prerequisite of successful revolutionary struggles.

Hence, by putting terrorism in command, POQO could not harness the rashness of violent reactions for purposes beyond their initial phase of isolated acts of desperate individuals. While POQO's terrorism may momentarily have intimidated the white ruling class, it failed on the main count: instead of bringing freedom in 1963, it signaled catastrophe.

It is not surprising that the ANC with its emphasis on political organization and its firm opposition to terrorism should have condemned the methods of POQO. Although violence had become a legitimate means in the struggle, "misguided violence or violence for its sake" was "unnecessary and senseless"; it could have "the gravest consequences for the movement." Accordingly the National Executive of the ANC advised POQO "against embarking on adventurous and futile acts of terrorism."[83]

Bram Fischer, the leader of the Communist Party, reflected the beliefs of the ANC and its left wing allies when he declared that "steady political work" and the campaign of sabotage would "without loss of life or injury to persons" make the "white voter in South Africa reconsider his whole attitude."[84] The campaign of sabotage was in this sense another form of protest; it was not conceived as a first step towards mass mobilization and revolution. It remained under the control of a conspiratorial elite characterized by its overall divorce from the exploited classes whose fortunes it sought to serve. This was the paradox of the early period of Umkhonto's violent resistance. The progressive relinquishment of peaceful forms of opposition was not accompanied by a basic shift in the world-view of the petty bourgeois leadership. Still convinced that it alone possessed the knowledge necessary for liberating black men and women, it remained essentially isolated from the masses.

Sabotage, with its highly technical gadgetry, was a sign of this isolation—it symbolized the barrier separating the leaders and the people. This absence of any dynamic contact with the exploited masses indicated the persistence of petty bourgeois convictions and precluded the development of a truly revolutionary movement.[85]

The failure to enlist mass energies in the struggle for liberation had disastrous consequences. The type of organization required for the campaign of sabotage was elitist and authoritarian to the extent that the task it set for itself was defined and led by a closely knit nucleus of professional cadres. When the police arrested these cadres in the white suburb of Rivonia on July 11, 1963, it neutralized and decapitated the revolutionary underground.[86] The masses who were left outside the arena of actions were now incapable of pursuing the struggle and defending their imprisoned leaders. The failure of the early transition to violence was symptomatic of the structural scission between the masses and their leaders.

This scission opened the door to a dangerous form of voluntarism. The conviction spread among the leaders that a military strategy relying on an elite corps of dedicated revolutionaries could rapidly shake and ultimately overthrow white supremacy. Such conviction dramatized a fatal if unconscious acceptance of the passivity of the masses. By negating the people's intervention in the revolutionary struggle, the national leadership demonstrated that its adoption of violent methods was not, as yet, the outcome of a rupture with petty bourgeois ideology and practices. This leadership was still not completely committed to its demise as a class. Such a transformation would have required the abandonment of sabotage as the method of struggle, and the rooting of military combat in the popular cultural and social setting. Ultimately, the success of the revolution depended on the power of the oppressed classes to make their own history.

If this structural divorce between leadership and masses was fundamentally responsible for undermining the first phase of modern armed resistance, there were other contributing factors. Among these was the difficulty embodied in the very transition from open and peaceful forms of protest to the politics of secrecy and violence. Indeed, the adoption of violence as a method of struggle was a traumatic experience for the petty bourgeois leadership. Forced to cut its roots with the long tradition of peaceful protests, this leadership was condemned to transform its morality, to change its way of life, and to abandon its modest but secure privileges.[87]

Not surprisingly, liberal critics of the militant wing of the liberation movement have argued that Albert Lutuli, the President of the ANC who was awarded the Nobel Peace Prize for his support for peaceful methods of resistance, opposed the turn to violence.[88] Yet, despite Lutuli's long standing advocacy of peaceful change, there is little to indicate that he rejected violence as an ultimate resort of liberation. In his Nobel Peace Prize address Lutuli declared that although "We, in our situation, have chosen the path of non-violence of our own volition . . . in some places armed force provoked by the adamancy of white rule, carries the only real promise of peace in Africa."[89] In light of this statement it is not surprising that Lutuli had warm words for the men of Umkhonto. After their condemnation to life imprisonment in June 1964, Lutuli issued a bitter declaration portraying them as "brave, just men" who could not be blamed "for seeking justice by the use of violent methods."

> Nor could they be blamed, [Lutuli added,] . . . if they tried to create an organized force in order to ultimately establish peace and racial harmony. . . . They represent the highest in morality and ethics in the South African political struggle, this morality and ethics has been sentenced to an imprisonment it may never survive.[90]

Hence, the contention that Lutuli and the "old guard" of the ANC opposed violence appears to have little substance. Moreover, the whole movement of African emancipation had by 1961 rejected its own past history of peaceful resistance. Liberals and communists, pan-Africanists and radicals became convinced of the regrettable necessity and inevitability of violent confrontation with the forces of white supremacy.[91] Despite their deep ideological differences, they were all united in their commitment to armed resistance. They were all forced to share Ted Honderich's notion that:

> Violence can be directed to undeniably good ends. . . . It can be directed to the changing of circumstances which are such, to describe them in one true way, that there will be a general agreement in the future that they were circumstances of moral barbarity. Violence can be directed . . . to ends which make for progress towards well-being for all people. . . . Violence, then, may serve the ends which are fundamental to the democratic practice . . . it may, as coercion, share an attribute with procedures that are intrinsic to democratic systems. It cannot be said without dismay and apprehension . . . that some bombs are like votes.[92]

If there was unity as to an understanding of the necessity for violence, there were major ideological differences between the ANC and the PAC. The ANC and Umkhonto were accused of becoming "Russian slaves"[93] and of diluting African nationalism with their policy of multiracialism. As the Africanist A. P. Mda declared: "The multi-racialist approach is negative. . . . It is not imbued with the spirit of disciplined positive action nor does it derive motive force from the mighty power of African Nationalism."[94] While it is true that a small group of white communists and radicals played an important and active role in formulating the political and military strategies of the ANC, it is difficult to fault this group for its commitment. It is also probably false to contend that its influence emasculated the black revolutionary struggle, although its advocacy of a nonracial and socialistic program certainly muted the stridency of African nationalism.

The nonracial approach of the ANC clearly contradicted Africanist and separatist conceptions, but it was an expression of both democratic principles and some elements of class analysis, and not a symbol of African inadequacy submitting to white arrogance. However, the insertion of whites in the top leadership of the liberation movement inhibited perhaps the full development of a national and popular revolutionary will. That whites could cut themselves off from their own racist roots to embrace the cause of African freedom contradicted the existing political reality to such a great extent that the masses must have looked skeptically at this generous democratic impulse.[95]

From this perspective, liberals and Africanists argued that the disproportionate influence of communists in the ANC made it impossible for it to lead the masses correctly. Communism, they maintained, had taken over the ANC and was using it as a front organization to establish a proletarian dictatorship.[96] That communists had closely collaborated with the ANC is indisputable and certainly not surprising since their ultimate vision of a classless society coincided at least initially with African objectives and aspirations for a just and nonracial South Africa.

While white communists and independent Marxists had contributed to the radicalization of the ANC, they certainly did not destroy the autonomy of African political thinking. The fact that the South African government would argue otherwise is not surprising given its tendency to subscribe to a form of racism which denies Africans the faculty of intellectual creativity. Communism was not forced on Africans; it became their natural ally in a common struggle, and if some blacks began to advocate its ideology, it was of their own volition. As Mandela explained:

> . . . experienced African politicians so readily accept Communists as their friends . . . [because] for many decades Communists were the only political group in South Africa who were prepared to eat with us; talk with us, live with us and work with us. They were the only political group which was prepared to work with the Africans for the attainment of political rights and a stake in society. Because of this, there are many Africans who, today, tend to equate freedom with Communism.[97]

Mandela denied that he ever was a member of the Communist Party; he regarded himself "in the first place, as an African patriot . . . influenced by Marxist thought."[98] The ideological commitment of the ANC, he declared, "is, and always has been, the creed of African Nationalism."[99] African nationalism, with its stress on the unity and harmony of black people of all classes and strata, was significantly different from communism which "sought to emphasize class distinction."[100]

Thus, whatever is to be said against violence, multiracialism and communism, there appears to be no significant substance to the argument that they constituted fundamental causes in the defeat of the first phase of modern armed resistance, and so should be rejected if the future of the revolution is to be assured. On the contrary, a radical transformation of South Africa requires the broadest possible opposition to white supremacy by widening the parameters of the struggle beyond race, and rooting it into a class theory. Such a scope is essential since the expansion of revolutionary practices leads to alternative political and cultural settings. More importantly, it challenges the petty bourgeoisie into accepting its demise as a class; it furthers the development of reformist nationalism into revolutionary nationalism; and it gradually materializes the rejection of elitism and capitalism into a socialist reality.

It is clear, however, that in the early 1960's the process of globalizing the struggle was only at an embryonic stage and it collapsed for several years with the arrest of the main leadership at Rivonia in 1963. Rivonia symbolized the other essential cause of the breakdown of the first phase of armed resistance: the saboteurs were too few, too overworked, and too inexperienced to confront the increasingly sophisticated, repressive machinery of the state.[101] As Thomas Karis argued:

> . . . the virtual destruction of the underground in 1963 was due not only to the amateurism of the saboteurs but also to the growing professionalism of the police. The Rivonia raid was not a lucky break but the culmination of a systematic build-up of counter-insurgency measures. Furthermore, during the nineteen months between Umkhonto's appearance and Rivonia, the government did much more than uproot most of the underground; it also demoralized and routed the radical opposition.[102]

Thus, the sudden decapitation of the internal revolutionary leadership whose raison d'être was to direct armed resistance created an inevitable political vacuum and engendered a profound sense of defeat in the African population. It is in this context that the Black Consciousness Movement began its ascendancy. The following chapters are a study of this movement and its growth. What needs to be briefly emphasized now, however, is the position of the Black Consciousness Movement in the ideological spectrum which separates Africanists from multiracialists.

While it is clear that the Black Consciousness Movement was deeply influenced by Africanism and developed an exclusionary policy towards whites, it nonetheless went beyond the confines of race and Africanness. Indeed, the notion of 'blackness' which decisively molded the Movement's outlook, was embedded in both the consequences of being black in a white supremacist state and he realities of material exploitation derived from a racial capitalism. As such, the concept 'black' came to encompass all of the exploited, irrespective of their Africanness. Asians and "Coloureds"—people of mixed racial descent—were previously regarded with skepticism and ambiguity by the Africanists, but were fully integrated into the Black Consciousness Movement provided they accepted their blackness. Moreover, the term 'black' was not attributed to all Africans. In fact, the Movement reserved the pejorative term 'non-white' to define those Africans, Asians and "Coloureds" who collaborated with white authorities. Accordingly, the Black Consciousness Movement condemned the African bureaucratic elite of the Bantustans for its incorporation into and acceptance of the political structures of apartheid.

Black Consciousness emphasized not merely race as a decisive factor in the struggle against white supremacy; it also stressed the interracial linkages preserving and enhancing the given racist reality. Thus, class as well as race occupied a privileged position in the BCM analysis of the South African social formation. In this sense, the BCM departed from the purely racial attitude and strategy of Africanism. Being African was not a sufficient condition to qualify as a black; to be black implied a determined antagonism to apartheid and the political will to eradicate it.

The white state, however, is bent on preventing the crystalization of such determined antagonism. Not only is it prepared to use force and violence, but it is also seeking to effect a "passive revolution," to borrow Antonio Gramsci's expression.[103] In other words, the managers of white supremacy are attempting to hold the subaltern African classes in a passive state by co-opting certain sections of the black leadership into a modified system of white domination. "Passive revolution" is thus a "revolution without a revolution."[104] That such a revolution is on the agenda of the white state at all is an indication that the continued domination of that state is no longer supported by hegemony. The relative passive consent which had characterized the politics of apartheid in the 1960's had vanished with the advent of the Black Consciousness Movement and consequently, the white state was forced to search for new policies and alliances with which it could reassert its hegemony. As Walter Adamson has explained:

> Passive revolution [becomes] attractive when a regime [possesses] domination but [lacks] hegemony and [needs] to curb a progressive force, preferably without any resort to violence, or at least without a protracted struggle. This [can] be accomplished by launching a minimally progressive political campaign designed to undercut the truly progressive classes. . .[105]

In the South African context such a minimally progressive campaign implied certain ideological, economic, and political departures from traditional apartheid. Indeed, if the coming to power of Afrikanerdom in 1948 symbolized the codification of racism with the institutionalization of segregation instead of its possible liberalization, it also created the terrain for the growth of black resistance. And it is precisely this resistance which has impelled white rulers to search for a new and more acceptable system of domination. Accordingly, the managers of white supremacy are engaged in a process of hegemonic de-racialization whereby certain concessions which do not endanger the existing structures of dominance are to be extended to the better-off sectors of the black population. As is demonstrated in chapter 6, the goal is to divide the opposition along class and ethnic lines and to integrate—in a subaltern position—certain parts of it into the white power network.

Hegemonic de-racialization represents not only the response of the white state to the new realities of vigorous black protests;

it is also a reaction to the novel and hostile constellation of power stemming from the collapse of the Portuguese colonial empire. The emergence of radical independent states in Angola and Mozambique has contributed to a new sense of urgency among white ruling circles. Indeed, hegemonic deracialization embodies the element of political concessions contained in what the defenders of apartheid have called the Total Strategy for white survival. The Total Strategy which was enunciated in the 1977 Defense White Paper, was designed to mobilize and co-ordinate all of South Africa's resources to face the challenge of "total war" created by this novel constellation of power. The challenge was all encompassing; it involved the military, political, cultural, economic, and psychological realms of life. Accordingly, the 1977 Defense White Paper advocated as essential the for-mulation of a "Total National Strategy" which implied a total system of defense.

> The defence of the Republic of South Africa is not solely the responsibility of the Department of Defence. On the contrary . . . [it] is the combined responsibility of all government departments. This can be taken further—it is the responsibility of the entire population, the nation and every population group.[106]

This required the militarization of society to cope with internal as well as external enemies; the implementation of hegemonic de-racialization to mollify black resistance; and the ascendancy of an "ideology of white survival" to facilitate the making of the "passive revolution." As Heribert Adam has remarked:

> The ideology of survival implies an unquestioned threat. . . . Survival means countering a challenge to life itself, the safety of sleeping securely at night.
> . . . Survival is thereby defined in biological terms; the survival of privileges need not be raised. Survival as well as identity represent respectable code words, vague enough to allow the leadership to manipulate their specific meaning. Yet they signal sufficient emo-tional appeal to rally the faithful behind those who promise relief from insecurity. . . .
> Survival politics allows the leadership to determine internal changes without laying itself open to charges of betrayal of doctrine. . . .[107]

It would be quite wrong, however, to assume that the ideology of survival can ensure the success of the passive revolution by displacing the entrenched racism nurtured by centuries of white domination. In other words, racism is so ingrained in the fabric of white South Africa that it is difficult to imagine how the moderate reforms embodied in passive revolution can mollify it, let alone abolish it. Moreover, a passive revolution in South Africa would attack not only the white system of beliefs, but it would also undermine the interests and privileges of wide sections of the white population. Accordingly, the implementation of the passive revolution is bound to generate opposition and contradictions within the white camp itself. The verkramptes ("hard-liners") will emphasize the intrinsic dangers of the passive revolution as it might open a Pandora's box and unfold a political dynamic which threatens instead of strengthens the structures of white supremacy. In addition, both the white bureaucracy, with its vested interest in the massive apparatus of apartheid, and the white working-class, with its acute resistance to the elimination of racially determined job-reservations, are likely to resist any passive revolution.[108]

Passive revolution, however, has gained the powerful support of the verligtes ("enlightened") faction of Afrikanerdom which dominates the current government of President P. W. Botha. Furthermore, the dominant sectors of South African capital, in their search for larger markets, skilled labor, and political stability, have promoted and solidified the position of the reformers. As Saul and Gelb have indicated:

> . . . the strengthening of the verligte position has been linked to the sea changes within the ranks of capital. . . . It reflects the gravitation of the emergent Afrikaner bourgeoisie toward a clearer meeting-of-minds with the multinational corporations and with the most developed (and now formidably diversified) segments of South African-based mining capital (e.g., Anglo American.) And this, in the context of the organic crisis, has meant a much stronger political basis for the "liberalization" of racial capitalism than existed in the 1940's.[109]

Such a political basis can be expected to consolidate itself further not only because of the power of capital, but also because of the military's support for passive revolution. Indeed, the military's strategy for winning over the black population implies a commitment to hegemonic de-racialization. Not surprisingly, the South African Defense Force (SADF) trained and deployed about 12,000 black troops between 1974 and 1979.[110] Such integration of blacks into the repressive apparatus of white supremacy served two main purposes. It enhanced the possibilities of a black against black confrontation and consequently, it introduced a further division in the ranks of the exploited majority, and, it strengthened the might of white supremacy by alleviating the shortage of manpower resources. In this sense, the military's support for the passive revolution is a clear indication that the quest for a new white hegemony is deeply implanted in the terrain of force and repression.

The fundamental point is that the circumstances which prompted the passive revolution were circumstances of insurrection and widespread discontent and therefore, of revolutionary potentialities and opportunities as well as of reactionary statecraft and violence. The diffusion of Black Consciousness undermined the hegemony of apartheid to such an extent that the defense of white supremacy came to rest almost exclusively on the use of brute force. This, however, reflected the contradictory nature of white power: it was indeed dominant since it resolved all disputes with the iron fist, but it was inherently weak since its very survival depended on the constant exercise of crude repression. And it is precisely because the cost of dominance without hegemony is prohibitive at the political, economic, and military levels that white supremacy has sought to restructure its method of governance. The passive revolution has become the means to that end. It is clearly not reasonable, however, to characterize it as a retreat from dominance and force. For the travail of the Black Consciousness Movement has eroded white hegemony to the point that any passive revolution in South Africa will have to be backed by the force of arms. In other words, the Black Consciousness Movement has created an alternative hegemony which can only be satisfied by the complete liberation of the black masses.

This, however, raises the issue of which strategy and means the BCM contemplated to achieve that liberation. Rooted in Christianity and the ideals of nonviolence, it envisaged liberation as a peaceful process of radical change. It was not until Soweto demonstrated the futility of such a peaceful process that the youngsters of the BCM began to contemplate the necessity of revolutionary violence. Even then, the espousal of revolutionary violence was not unanimous. Five to seven thousand members of the BCM, however, left South Africa in the aftermath of Soweto to join the exile organizations, principally the ANC.

This exodus did not imply a complete ideological congruity between the exclusiveness of Black Consciousness and the multiracialism of the ANC. In fact, the issue of white participation in the struggle against apartheid, and the close relations between the ANC and the Communist Party of South Africa (CPSA) became sources of tension and friction between the youngsters of Soweto and the exiled leadership. However, these conflicts, which will be examined in a subsequent chapter, did not result in a new and fundamental scission of African resistance, but they were reminders of the perennial and divisive question of white participation in the struggle against white supremacy.

The issue of white participation inevitably contains the problem of race and class and the distinctive ideological and political alternatives that it entails. The succeeding chapters of this book are an analysis of the Black Consciousness Movement's struggle to resolve this problem and chart a new framework of ideological resistance to white supremacy.

Chapter II

Ideology,
The Black Consciousness
Movement, and Social Change
in South Africa

The ideological manifestations of the Black Consciousness Movement are essential to any understanding of contemporary South Africa, for the content of this consciousness will have a lasting and decisive impact on the unfolding political and revolutionary struggle, as well as on the institution of a racially liberated South Africa. Indeed, such consciousness is a source of moral anger and self-affirmation which embodies an ethical and political standard that condemns the existing social order and offers the vision of an alternative society. Without such consciousness the likelihood of a comprehensive and sustained African challenge to white supremacy is remote. Structural changes in South Africa hinge upon the erosion of the relative legitimacy of white domination and on the defeat of the sense of inevitability supporting the exploitation of the black people. For, as Barrington Moore has argued:

People are evidently inclined to grant legitimacy to anything that is or seems inevitable no matter how painful it may be. Otherwise the pain might be intolerable. The conquest of this sense of inevitability is essential to the development of politically effective moral outrage. For this to happen, people must perceive and define their situation as the consequence of human injustice: a situation that they need not, cannot, and ought not to endure. By itself of course such a perception, be it a novel awakening or the content of hallowed tradition, is no guarantee of political and social changes to come. But without some very considerable surge of moral anger such changes do not occur.[1]

The Black Consciousness Movement contributed to such a surge of moral anger; its radicalization became an indispensable spur to black revolutionary activity. The development of Black Consciousness as a counter-consciousness, channeling the unified opposition of the black population to the dominance of the white core, became a fundamental and necessary ingredient in the process of challenging white supremacy. As long as the ideological terrain—in which perceptions of the world take root and grow to limit or extend the range of historical alternatives—remains the uncontested territory of the racial myth, few if any structural transformations can be expected.

These structural transformations hinge upon the overall negation of the process of social reproduction. Initially such a negation assumes an ideological character which imparts a new moral and ethical vision of the feasible to the human subject. Goran Therborn has put this well in arguing that ideology consists of a threefold 'interpellation' of the individual:

1. Ideological formation tells individuals what exists, who they are, how the world is, how they are related to that world. In this manner, people are allocated different kinds and amounts of identity, trust and everyday knowledge. The visibility of modes of life, the actual relationship of performance to reward, the existence, extent and character of exploitation and power are all structured in class-specific modes of ideological formation.

2. Ideology tells what is possible, providing varying types and quantities of self-confidence and ambition, and different levels of aspiration.

3. Ideology tells what is right and wrong, good and bad, thereby determining not only conceptions of legitimacy of power, but also

work-ethics, notions and leisure, and views of interpersonal relationships, from comradeship to sexual love.[2]

Hence, the importance of ideology cannot be minimized. While ideology may be functional to the exigencies of the South African capitalist mode of production, it need not be so. There may develop among the subordinate classes a counter-ideology, a prophetic ideology, which not only fails to correspond to these exigencies, but also contributes to the general dislocation of the social order. This general dislocation brought about by the convulsions of the ideological realm opens the avenues for profound structural transformations. This is not to say that the capitalist mode of production has no distinctive or limiting effect on the formation of this counter-ideology, but rather to maintain that in the revolutionizing of society, the counter-ideology of the subordinate classes weakens the power of the ruling class and propels society toward a revolutionary predicament.

Ideology in this sense must be considered as the expressive means through which men and women make their own history as conscious agents. This does not mean that ideology is completely independent from material conditions, but that it has an autonomy of its own which in turn conditions the historical transformation of the mode of production. This study therefore rejects the notion, put forward by what might be called deterministic Marxism[3] that ideology refers to false consciousness— as opposed to true consciousness which corresponds to a 'scientific' understanding of reality.

Ideology, in the deterministic Marxian universe, is the effective form of consciousness which fails to correspond to the real interests of the historical agents, since it is antithetical to their class interests. Thus, because deterministic Marxism is based on the principle that human behavior is determined by class interest, anything which does not coincide with these interests must by necessity be false consciousness; that is, it must be ideology. In this sense, what determines true human motivation is class interests which in turn are determined by the existing economic structures. As a result, culture and human action itself become the mere epiphenomena of the economic mode of production.

Such deterministic Marxism is marked by the absence of dialectical analysis, and this tends to transform it into a mechanistic materialism in which the capitalist mode of production inexorably determines all aspects of social life. In this theory there is little space for culture, psychology, and human passions as autonomous spheres imparting certain qualities to historical development. The unilateral stress on the overpowering impact of capitalist structures, as they make and shape society, negates the anthropomorphic dimension of social change and revolution.

While capitalist structures impose definite constraints and limits to human behavior and cultural transformation, there is no reason to believe that both are pure reflections and emanations of these structures. If this were so, capitalist civilization would be permanent and eternal, since it would forever reproduce the overall conditions of its existence. In brief, the remorseless, mechanistic materialism of deterministic Marxism has, when applied to South Africa, the unintended effect of making racism and capitalism unmovable and unshakable structures of exploitation.[4] This not only restricts the analytical range of historical alternatives, it also does violence to the very corpus of Marxist theory. For, as Eugene Genovese has pointed out:

> The strength of Marxian materialism, relative to other materialism, is its dialectic, which gives it, or ought to give it . . . flexibility and wholeness. . . . The principle of interrelatedness is fundamental to Hegelian and Marxian dialectics and cannot be sacrificed to convenient notions of simple causation. If dialectical materialism is taken seriously, it must assert historical continuity as well as discontinuity. Every historical event necessarily embraces the totality of its components, each of which brings to that event the product of its total historical development. For this reason alone, a failure to respect the force of a people's tradition and historically developed sensibility will always prove fatal to materialist thought and betray it into mechanism. . . . A convincing materialism is to account for the complexity of societies in their historical uniqueness and for the special manifestations of the human spirit.[5]

It is precisely because deterministic Marxism failed to take into account these "special manifestations of the human spirit" that its materialism collapses into a mechanistic materialism. Deterministic Marxism may be right in asserting that the development of racism as a full blown belief-system of white superordination and black subordination is rooted in the material base of early capitalistic expansion;[6] but there is no justification for its claim that such racism cannot achieve an autonomy of its own and that it is a permanent emanation of the capitalist mode of production. With the passage of time, racism has become so deeply woven into the texture of South African life that its survival is now no longer dependent on continuous capitalist nurturings. In fact, its enduring and pervasive character imposes serious constraints on the development of industrial capitalism. It also introduces significant contradictions between the different factions of white capital.

Indeed, from a strict economic point of view, apartheid has contributed to a less than optimum productive system since the industrial color-bar which reserves the best jobs for white workers has created a shortage of skilled labor. Moreover, the exploitation of the black working class has limited the expansion of the market. Yet, these constraints on the development of capitalism have had a contradictory impact on the different sectors of capital. Accordingly, the political strategies of these different sectors have varied.

Industrial capital has tended to envisage the defense of its class interests as the progressive liberalization of apartheid through the granting of certain privileges and concessions to urban Africans. Small and agricultural capitals on the other hand, have hoped to preserve the existing reality because their dependence on cheap African labor clashes with the emergence of trade unions and a larger African wage bill. The racist hierarchical division of labor is a source of tension and friction between the different sectors of capital; also, it imposes clear limitations on the scope and nature of any future process of de-racialization. As Robert Davies has explained:

> The fact that the classes represented by the governing party have a number of vital fractional interest whose continued realization remains quite critically dependent upon their maintaining their

political position, means that even though these classes may now
be more willing and able to tolerate the granting of certain economic
concessions to blacks or even to incorporation of certain black
dominated classes in subordinate places within the state apparatuses,
they cannot afford to tolerate any restructuring of political class
relations which might threaten their particular place in the state.
They must above all resist any neo-colonial type "majority rule"
solution which could lead to their displacement as [a] governing
class . . . [and this] places severe limitations on the capacity of
the [white] power bloc as currently organised to stabilise political
class relations and fundamentally alter South Africa's current position as a crisis ridden weak link in the imperialist chain.[7]

Racism, then, as the protective shield of the class interests of
certain elements of white capital and as a profoundly ingrained
tradition of thought and behavior, imparts a decisive dimension
to the South African social structure and mode of production,
both of which cease to be—if they ever were—the sole and
independent agencies of history. Apartheid is not only the
capitalist mechanism supplying a vast army of cheap African
labor to the white economy; it is also a manifestation of the
cultural realm as embedded in the white racialist ethos. Capitalist
exploitation and class privilege do not require a racialist structure; labor repressive systems have been the universal hallmark
of the period of early industrialization and they embody most
contemporary experience of Third World modernization.

While capitalism made a major contribution to the formation
of apartheid, there is no unilateral connection between the two.
That exploitation and domination assumed a racialist dimension
cannot simply be explained in terms of capitalist exigencies.
Rather, race as a means of mobilization in the defense of
privilege and supremacy provided the white masses with something real and incomparably superior to a still nascent and
conflict-ridden class consciousness. White racism is not just a
"false consciousness"; however deplorable, it held the immediate
promise of material prosperity and cultural superiority.

Consequently, rather than being an epiphenomenon of the
capitalist mode of production, racism epitomizes a process of
ecological differentiation which systematically deprecates black
human beings to exclude them from the whites' moral com-

munity. As such, Africans are transformed into objects of exploitation to be manipulated as mere factors of production. While this particular set of arrangements has been functional to the capitalist extraction of an economic surplus, it is not all there is to racism. For, this racism has generated a white ethos that has imparted a moral and cultural inferiority to the black population and conditions the very development of capitalism. It is precisely because racism was such an active ideological force encroaching on the material base of society, that the South African political economy developed as a Volkskapitalisme.

Volkskapitalisme is not a pure system of class appropriation of the economic surplus, that fact in itself distinguishes it from the classical mode of capitalist production. Volkskapitalisme is a social system in which a racially determined hegemonic core, controlling the state, drains the economic surplus from a racially determined subordinate periphery. The term hegemonic core refers to a dominant power bloc uniting at the economic, political, and ideological levels, different classes sharing a common interest in the preservation of white supremacy.

This unity does not prevent the existence of certain contradictions between the classes. However, these contradictions are not fundamental; they founder in the defense of the wider corporate privilege. In contradistinction, the subordinate periphery forms an exploited pool of cheap labor which is legally and institutionally excluded from the political system and whose group solidarity is continuously fragmented, not only by the elemental predicament of survival, but also by specific state policies.

In the South African case, the Afrikaners captured political power and used the state to legalize the racial and economic exploitation of the African labor force. Such exploitation is expressed in the structures of inequality which have shown through the years a resilient persistence despite considerable economic growth and urbanization. In 1917 the African share of the total income was 18 percent; it rose by only 2 percent to 20 percent in 1970. The per capita ratio of white to African income increased from 13.2:1 to 15.2:1 during the same period.

In addition, South Africa has probably the world's most inegalitarian pattern of income distribution: in 1976 the top 20 percent of income earners received 71 percent of total income, and with a Gini coefficient of 0.65, South Africa is the society coming closer to "complete inequality."[8] The gap between white and African incomes is thus a massive chasm: in 1975 the African percapita income was estimated at between 200 rands and 250 rands, while that of the white population was 2,500 rands.[9] These circumstances have led Stanley Greenberg to conclude that "there is little prospect that economic growth, even under the most optimistic assumptions, will fundamentally alter the economic inequalities characteristic of South Africa."[10]

The South African economic predicament is not limited to these grim figures of persistent inequality; it extends into the field of African unemployment. While estimates of African unemployment vary greatly—from 10 to 25 percent of the labor force, they clearly indicate that it increased during the 1970's and will continue to do so in the 1980's, even under optimistic economic forecasts. Rapid population increases are partly responsible for this high level of unemployment. While it is projected that the annual employment growth rate for manufacturing will be 2.3 percent between 1978 and 1987, the annual increase of the labor force is placed at 2.6 percent for the same period.[11] Population growth will therefore contribute to the aggravation of unemployment.

Capital deepening—the process whereby industrial production expands beyond consumer goods to include capital goods employed in the production of consumer goods themselves—is also a major factor in the exacerbation of the labor surplus problem. Indeed, the type of technology used in South Africa is essentially capital intensive and labor saving, and is consequently ill equipped to reduce the growing black army of unemployed. Hence, there is no compelling evidence to support the thesis that rapid economic growth has significantly bettered the African condition.

The exploitation of the African periphery, however, is not limited exclusively to economics. It is also reflected in the degrading conditions of urban life in the townships where a massive housing shortage condemns Africans to crude over-crowding and nonexistent hygiene:

> In 1980 the government estimated the total housing shortfall for blacks at 40,000 units. The Urban Foundation has estimated it at more than 500,000. . . . A sample survey of houses in Soweto in 1979 revealed that only 5.8 percent of the houses had inside baths, and only 12.8 percent had inside toilets. Twenty one percent had running (cold) water inside the houses. Fewer than 20 percent of Soweto's houses have electricity. Most homes have coal or wood stoves, accounting for the pall of smoke that usually hangs over much of the township.[12]

If the African urban condition is miserable, it nonetheless compares well to that prevailing in the Bantustans—the ten geographical areas comprising about 13 percent of South Africa's territory in which Africans are supposed to obtain their rights of self-determination. A study of poverty in the Transkei, the most comprehensively examined of all Bantustans, reveals that in the late 1960's

> no less that 85 percent of households received an income below the Poverty Datum Line (PDL—defined as the theoretical absolute minimum requirement of a family to stay alive in the short term) . . . [Moreover] nearly 30 percent of children in the Transkei's rural districts die before they reach the age of 2, 40 percent before the age of ten—as a direct or indirect result of malnutrition.[13]

More evidence of impoverishment could be easily cited, but the point is already clear: the black population of South Africa constitutes an exploited periphery of labor.

It is on such exploitation that rested the foundations of Volkskapitalisme and the restoration of the organic unity of Afrikanerdom, a unity which dissolved the nascent, multiracial proletariat of the 1930's and 1940's. The emergence of Volks-kapitalisme in South Africa required therefore a conjuncture of economic and cultural forces resulting in three different but interrelated phenomena: the dissolution of the process of mul-tiracial proletarianization induced by British-led industrialization; the subsequent re-creation of the organic unity of the Afrikaner 'nation'; and the cultural and ethical differentiation of the Africans as an exploitable periphery.[14]

Indeed, during the 1930's and 1940's the development of British-led capitalism had divided the Afrikaner 'nation'. Class interests were gradually replacing ethnic solidarity, proletarian uncertainties and miseries were undermining the self-reliant existence of the platteland, and urban life was eroding religious beliefs and Calvinist norms. How to arrest the disintegration of Afrikanerdom and how to restore its cultural and material integrity became the central preoccupation of Afrikaner nationalists.[15]

The key to the resolution of this crisis rested on the eradication of white poverty which became a dangerous catalyst for class mobilization and a corrosive agent of ethnic identification and unity. Such an enormous task, however, required massive state intervention in the economy; this in turn necessitated the Afrikaner conquest of political power. The regeneration of the ethnic, linguistic, and material bonds which attached the individual Afrikaner to his or her 'national' Volk community and cemented the organic unity of Afrikanerdom became the means to that end. Hence, Afrikaner leaders pursued at least three major and interrelated objectives: the elimination of white poverty; the conquest of political power; and the spiritual revival of Afrikanerdom. Each involved the deepening of ever-present anti-British and anti-black sentiments and each fostered ethnic exclusiveness and pride as a means to weaken the emerging sense of class-belonging and class interests.

Ethnic and racist interpellations dissolved class divisions and regenerated the peculiar consciousness of Afrikanerdom. Yet, Afrikaner nationalists clearly realized that the unity of their "ethnie"[16] could not be sustained by culture alone, and that such unity would remain fragile and indeed illusory until it rooted itself in a strong material base. While the creation of this material base hinged upon the massive intervention of the state in the economy, it never embodied an alternative to, but on the contrary an ethnicitization of, capitalism. Afrikaner nationalists sought to accommodate their proposals for social change to the limits of adaptability within the prevailing capitalist order.

Afrikaner nationalists demanded a prompt end to the unregulated market economy, which in effect, condemned a large number of the Volk to the misery of a decaying agricultural sector or the harsh conditions of proletarian life. The state was to intervene in the economy to foster the growth of Afrikaner capital, and to create a strong Afrikaner bourgeoisie and labor aristocracy. Capitalism was to be transformed into a Volskapitalisme.[17] As Professor E. P. DuPlessie, an ideologue of Afrikanerdom, put it:

> The purpose of our economic struggle is thus national, even Christian National, as against the personal and sectional. As organized Afrikanerdom, we wish consciously to take part in the economic development of our land, naturally in order to ensure our own existence, but above all to restore our People to Prosperity and so enable it to fulfill its God-given calling. . . . [In the past] we accepted as inevitable that the masses who were unable to adjust [to capitalism] quickly or well enough should drop to poor-whiteism. Sympathetically we belittled them and separated ourselves from them, or at best offered them "alms" in a philanthropic manner. . . . Meantime this process of adjustment was destroying our People by denationalization of its economic leaders and proletarianization of its producing masses. But in the awakening of self-consciousness the People had become aware of this also, and the new ethnic movement is intended to prevent the further destruction of the Afrikaner People in an effort to adjust to a foreign capitalist system, and intends rather to mobilize the People to conquer this system and to transform it so that it fits our ethnic nature.[18]

Seen in this light, Afrikanerdom is neither anticapitalist, nor does it represent an irrational ethos bent on reproducing the pristine lifestyle of the platteland. On the contrary, it sets itself to develop a Volskapitalisme that assures the material prosperity of the ethnie in the modern and urban setting of bourgeois production. That the state has played a formative role in the institutionalization of this Volskapitalisme is by no means an indication that Afrikanerdom has departed from the capitalist path. On the contrary, state intervention in the private economy embodied not only the sole realistic alternative for the growth of Afrikaner capital in the face of British economic supremacy, but it has been a classical feature of all forms of late-capitalist industrialization as the cases of Germany and Japan attest. Yet, it remains true that the pervasiveness of the racist objective of state intervention in South Africa is unique in the history of contemporary capitalism.

However, it would be quite wrong to assume that the racist structures of production are forever frozen or rigidly anchored in the economic system. While the ideological goal of apartheid is segregation and separate territorial development of the races, there is nothing in it that contradicts the exploitation and use of black labor. The real rationale of apartheid is still encapsulated in what is known as the Stallard Commission of 1922, which inspired the long list of legislations regulating the lives of urbanized Africans. The Commission determined that the privileges of urbanization and industrialization were to be the exclusive preserve of the white community. In other words, racial segregation was to be encouraged as long as it did not conflict with the requirements of the white economy. The whole concept is embodied in what has been called the Stallard dictum of principle:

> We consider that the history of the races, especially having regard to South African history, shows that the commingling of black and white is undesirable. The Native should only be allowed to enter urban areas, which are essentially the White man's creation, when he is willing to enter and to minister to the needs of the white man, and should depart there from when he ceases to so minister.[19]

Thus, apartheid is an oppressive system of labor exploitation determined by a particular pattern of class domination expressed and shaped by racial and ethnic criteria. Volkskapitalisme refers to a peculiar form of capitalist exploitation embodied in the ethnic appropriation of the economic surplus generated by cheap black labor. The principal objective of Volkskapitalisme is not so much the promotion of an Afrikaner bourgeoisie, although such a promotion was instrumental in the development of Volkskapitalisme itself, but the preservation and expansion of the material base of white supremacy.

In these circumstances it would be foolish to deny the structural importance of racism to the white hegemonic core as a whole. The discriminatory and segregationist aspects of capitalist production are congruent with the general interests of white South Africans. However, these discriminatory and segregationist aspects of production do undergo changes if continued economic growth so requires—a process of adaptation which is amply demonstrated by the flexible application of the color-bar.

This flexibility, however, is not a prelude to the imminent collapse of white supremacy, nor does it represent the corrosive impact of capitalist industrialization on the system of racial stratification. Rather, as David Mason has argued, it

> . . . derives in large measure not from the triumph of economic pressures over a 'statism' rooted in traditional racial ideologies, but from the essential pragmatism of a state apparatus which has always been concerned to foster economic progress as a means, inter alia, of protecting white employment.[20]

Moreover, it is not just that the flexibility of the job color-bar is functional to the employment policies of Volkskapitalisme, but that it is compatible with low labor costs. There is nothing in the upward movement of the color-bar which entails a necessary increase in black wages. The channeling of white jobs into a multitude of less skilled processes of production performed by black workers for much lower wages represents the common mode of devaluing the black labor market, even as workers increase their job-skills. But the degradation of white jobs has not only the effect of cheapening the overall pattern of production. It has also, and more importantly, racially divided the processes of conception and execution.

Conception, or the intellectual component of the system of production, is increasingly concentrated in and monopolized by white workers, while execution, or the manual component of this system of production, is exclusively performed by the vast African proletariat.[21] The development of secondary industry in South Africa has not conflicted with segregationist and discriminatory industrial structures. Rather, apartheid and capitalist structures have been flexible enough to assure both the continued material prosperity of white supremacy and the continued racial stratification of the labor force. Accordingly, with its coming to power in 1948 the nascent Afrikaner bourgeoisie acquired the means for its more rapid development and consolidation.

The introduction into the already segregated social structure of the labor repressive and nonmarket apartheid system rationalized the extraction of the economic surplus from the African periphery, institutionalized the privileged position of the white hegemonic core, and legitimized the exclusion of the African periphery from the political community of the white power bloc.[22] Apartheid also helped to define the class character of society by progressively merging British and Afrikaner industrial bourgeoisies into a truly national capitalist class committed to the continuity of its own interests and the supremacy of the hegemonic core over the subjugated African periphery. Afrikaner and British industrial capitals have developed increasingly similar interests and visions. As Heribert Adam has remarked in his study of Afrikaner power:

> The new class of Afrikaner businessmen has deepened the cleavages within the Afrikaner establishment by making common cause with their English counterparts against preindustrial apartheid practices. However, at the same time a greater measure of unity between the English economic elite and Afrikaner political elite has manifested itself. English and Afrikaner elites are now able to interpenetrate each other. . . . While political decision making still takes place within the Afrikaner context and the English have by no means all joined the Nationalists or, for that matter, would be accepted, the mutual collaboration of decisive individuals from both camps has increased considerably.[23]

This concentration of white economic power has contributed to the emergence of a racist world-view which has facilitated the reproduction of class and racial relations. In fact, this world-view has permeated the colonial-settler community to such an extent and has been projected so powerfully by the white state's manipulation of communications[24] that it has become hegemonic[25] in important sectors of the African periphery. It has influenced the behavior and attitude of both the core and the periphery.

Hence, the hegemonic core has succeeded in persuading a significant number of Africans to accept its own cultural ethos and values. By establishing this intellectual and moral hegemony, the core has minimized its use of violence, partly legitimized its rule, and obtained the passive consent of elements within the African periphery. Yet, it would be wrong to exaggerate the extent of the legitimacy of white power. While white supremacy rested significantly on its capacity to establish its intellectual and moral hegemony over the African periphery, this hegemony in turn depended on the repressive potential of the white state and indeed on the unleashing of this potential in periods of political crises. Thus, to use Antonio Gramsci's phrase, white hegemony is "protected by the armor of coercion." The passive consent of the African population resulted from the complex interrelationship between white cultural and educational hegemony and the ever-present threat of the state's decisive and massive use of brutal force.

This is not to say that passive consent is an all-embracing and totally pervasive feature of the African periphery. On the contrary, African challenges to white ideological predominance have always eroded that predominance and opened up cracks in the hegemonic wall of white supremacy. In such moments of hegemonic difficulty repression and violence become *the* means of white rule. Thus, while the relative hegemony of white supremacy minimized the direct use of force, it was never powerful enough to squash black resistance and gain the full consent of the African masses.

A certain amount of consent, however, has shaped and defined some African interests in such a manner as to make them partly congruent with racial domination. Such consent deriving from the white dominated 'production of consciousness' has always been linked to the prestige and status which the hegemonic core has enjoyed as a result of its dominant function and position in the realm of material production. In a memorable passage, Marx and Engels explained this "production of consciousness" as follows:

> The ideas of the ruling class are in every epoch the ruling ideas; i.e., the class, which is the ruling material force of society is at the same time its ruling intellectual force. The class which has the means of material production at its disposal, has control at the same time over the means of mental production, so that thereby, generally speaking, the ideas of those who lack the means of mental production are subject to it. The ruling ideas are nothing more than the ideal expression of the dominant material relationships, the dominant material relationships grasped as ideas; hence of the relationships which make the one class the ruling one, therefore the ideas of its dominance. The individuals composing the ruling class possess among other things consciousness, and therefore think. In so far, therefore, as they rule as a class and determine the extent and compass of an epoch, it is self-evident that they do this in their whole range, hence among other things rule also as thinkers, as producers of ideas, and regulate the production and distribution of the ideas of their age: thus their ideas are the ruling ideas of the epoch.[26]

Yet, the central point remains, that the ideological hegemony of the core can neither by itself preserve the relative stability of the South African Volkskapitalisme, nor sustain the system of white supremacy. Since the African periphery is reduced to the status of a mere commodity from which the core extracts its economic surplus, a polarized and antagonistic social structure is bound to emerge. In short, a clear-cut polarization between the African periphery and the hegemonic core, in the long run, generates the unified resistance of the former to the extractive policies of the latter. Consequently, the unchecked development of this structural polarization creates a conjuncture favorable to the eventual disintegration of the colonial settler system as the African periphery struggles to a new consciousness and overwhelms the hegemonic core.

Bent on preserving its privileges without resorting to the massive use of violence and terror, the core has, to date, centered its energies on the creation of an African semi-periphery of 'honorary whites' in order to thwart the potential unified resistance of the periphery. While suffering the exploitation of the core, this semi-periphery shares—albeit unequally and yet sufficiently—in the exploitation of the periphery and so constitutes a most important factor in the de-polarization of the colonial-settler system. It is in light of these factors that one must understand the creation of Bantustans with their own black elites and the limited concessions made to some sectors of the urban African population.[27]

The Bantustans are no longer just reservoirs of cheap African labor. They have become an acid ravaging the potential unification of the African periphery and the logical territory for the development of increasing class differentiations. Thus, the Bantustanization of the African periphery is primarily a process of 'ethno-nation-building.' This is grounded in the formation of semi-peripheral African bourgeoisies bent on furthering their own class interests through the consolidation of their respective ethno-nations.[28] The Bantustans—as potential ethno-nations peripheral to the core—serve to dissolve the cultural and economic unity of the African periphery by dividing it into a multiplicity of nascent and antagonistic ethno-nations controlled by semi-peripheral African bourgeoisies. As Immanuel Wallerstein has observed:

> . . . the formation of an "ethno-nation" serves to alter the distribution of goods according to some arbitrarily defined "status"—kinship, language, race, religion, citizenship. Ethno-nations defend or seek to acquire privilege through partial or total monopolies, distinguishing the group and creating organizational cohesion by the manipulation of cultural symbols.
>
> Ethno-national consciousness is the constant resort of all those for whom class organization offers the risk of a loss of relative advantage through the normal workings of the market and class dominated political bargaining. It is obvious that this is frequently the case for upper strata, who thereby justify differential reward on one or another version of racist ideology. Furthermore, insofar as dominant groups can encourage a generalized acceptance of ethno-nationalism as a base for political action, they precisely achieve the three-tiered structure of exploitation which helps maintain the stability of the system.[29]

The study of the Black Consciousness Movement as a counter-ideology of resistance to white supremacy is essential to any understanding of contemporary South Africa. For this consciousness and the forms and shapes that it has assumed will eventually condition the future situation of black women and men. The evolving nature of the Black Consciousness Movement will also impart a conciliatory or revolutionary, a peaceful or violent, a bourgeois or socialist dimension to the confrontation between blacks and whites. By eschewing violence and emphasizing black cultural and psychological emancipation from white hegemony—to the relative neglect of economic issues—the Black Consciousness Movement was *initially* the vehicle of a black philosophy of pride and self-affirmation invigorated by an ethic of "Christian Liberation."

Thus, the Black Consciousness Movement embodied the ideals of Negritude and the Christian message of salvation—the beginnings of the Kingdom of God to be struggled for here on earth as well as enjoyed in Heaven. The Black Consciousness Movement opposed the white ascendancy of apartheid on a cultural plane and it stressed self-help and the encouragement of cultural organizations. However, it gradually developed an understanding of the material conditions of life, and as such the Movement became much more than a mere cultural renaissance. While Black Consciousness drew its early inspiration from both Negritude and Christianity, it came to recognize the phenomenon of class struggle and the fundamental role of man in abolishing oppressive social structures. While the degradation and dehumanization of the black person by white racism generated a reactive African consciousness which asserted the intrinsic worth of black people and black culture, the social gospel of a radical Christianity—a theology of liberation—encouraged the tradition of African communalism while identifying with the poor against the exploitative structures of apartheid.

Indeed, since it developed against both the structures of capitalist exploitation and the dehumanizing culture of white racism, the Black Consciousness Movement crystalized as a synthesis of class awareness and black cultural assertiveness. The result was a prophetic Christianity envisaging and promoting the just society of the future. The Movement, however, with its emphasis on black culture, identity and self-love, could not by itself destroy the system of entrenched white privilege. While psychological emancipation from white supremacy was a fundamental and necessary stage for political action, it tended to become an end in itself and to develop into a poor substitute for revolutionary strategy.

Examining Black Consciousness as an ideology capable of challenging the cultural hegemony of the white supremacist regime entails understanding the Movement as the ethico-political[30] weapon of an oppressed class struggling to reaffirm its humanity through active participation in the demise of a racist and capitalist system. As such, the Black Consciousness Movement was a philosophy of praxis that attempted to eradicate from the black intellect the inculcated submissiveness that contributed to its own enslavement. Consequently, the Movement directed great attention to the problem of the superstructure, for it asserted that the liberation of the black people would begin only when their mental constructs of their own inferiority ceased to guide their historical conduct. The black revolution which the material structure made latent could only be activated by the transformation of the black intellect. Thus, the revolution would occur only if the black mind stripped itself from submission to white hegemony and erected on its own foundations the principles of the new moral order.

The Black Consciousness Movement was therefore bent on effecting what Antonio Gramsci described as an intellectual and moral reform. This reform is a profound cultural transformation which changes the masses' conception of life, politics, and economics. Accordingly, it ushers in a new social and moral vision and it restructures the role and place of the hitherto subordinate and dominant classes. Such massive transformation embodies the "cathartic moment" of liberation whereby the "structure ceases to be an external force which crushes man, assimilates him to itself and makes him passive; and is transformed into a means of freedom, an instrument to create a new ethico-political form and a source of new initiatives."[31]

The "cathartic moment," however, is neither spontaneous nor mechanical; it requires the dissemination of a new hegemony and hence the emergence of a new intellectual elite. This elite constitutes the thinking and organizing group of intellectuals who articulate the programmatic aspirations of one of the fundamental classes of society. Accordingly, these intellectuals clarify the ideas and objectives of the class to which they are organically linked.[32] They contribute to the transition of a class in itself into a class for itself. Therefore, the organic intellectuals are in fact the bearers of a new and potentially revolutionary self-consciousness. In Gramsci's words:

> Critical self-consciousness means, historically and politically, the creation of an "elite" of intellectuals. A human mass does not "distinguish" itself, does not become independent in its own right without in the widest sense, organising itself; and there is no organisation without intellectuals, that is without organisers and leaders, in other words, without the theoretical aspect of the theory-practice nexus being distinguished concretely by the existence of a group of people "specialised" in conceptual and philosophical elaboration of ideas. But the process of creating intellectuals is long, difficult, full of contradictions, advances and retreats, dispersals and regroupings, in which the loyalty of the masses is often sorely tried.[33]

It is this complex and difficult process of intellectual renewal and creativity which fundamentally characterized the Black Consciousness Movement. The youngsters who comprised the Movement represented the ascending organic intellectuals of the coming black revolution.

Thus, it would be wrong to equate the Black Consciousness Movement with a mere cultural renaissance; it was indeed more than that. Black Consciousness recognized the centrality of the material conditions of existence and it was precisely because of these that it rejected collaboration with whites—however well intentioned they may have been. Because whites did not experience first-hand and could not 'feel' the predicament of being black—not simply because of their pigmentation, but above all because of their exclusive and abusive bourgeois privileges—they could not join in the struggle of the black masses. Being black was not determined by color alone; it was determined by the daily experience of enduring oppression as a class of exploited peasants and urban workers. A white could sympathize with a black, yet economic advantages almost inexorably kept him white; as such, he remained at best a paternalistic reformer and at worst, a conscious exploiter.

If the economic structures of apartheid maintained white minority solidarity, they tended to divide blacks into opposing but not necessarily antagonistic strata.[34] In their endeavor to preserve their newly acquired status of wealth and power, blacks of the urban petty bourgeoisie[35] and especially those of the Bantustans' administrative elite, strove to become whites. Yet, always emasculated and rejected by white racists they degenerated into a particular hybrid—the 'non-whites.' The non-whites emulated everything white and repudiated everything black. They were, in Tawney's terminology, the "tadpoles" of history, for they thought that it was possible to

> . . . reconcile themselves to the inconveniences of their position, by reflecting that, though most of them will live and die as tadpoles and nothing more, the more fortunate of the species will one day shed their tails, distend their mouths and stomachs, hop nimbly on to dry land, and croak addresses to their former friends on the virtues by means of which tadpoles of character and capacity can rise to be frogs. . . . As though the noblest use of exceptional powers were to scramble to shore, undeterred by the thought of drowning companions![36]

Obviously this concept represented a false conception of apartheid society, for to become a frog in contemporary South Africa the tadpole would have to be born white. Tawney's tadpole philosophy sustained the belief in the possibility of material advancement through unfettered personal achievement—though it offered little of either. For a small black elite, it provided a way out of the misery engendered by a racist capitalism. It did not matter that few Africans escaped from poverty; those who failed to do so had only themselves to blame. Deeply etched in the black intellect, these myths helped to support and even legitimize economic disparities and white supremacy. No wonder that, bent as it was on transforming the social awareness of black men and black women, the Movement sought to destroy the hegemony of the bourgeois tadpole philosophy. Black Consciousness aimed at transforming the stultifying white colonial theology into a black theology of liberation and, therefore, it attempted to instill in the black intellect a radical ideology of hope—an ideology without which the recovery of black self-respect and humanhood was impossible.

This preoccupation with the creation of an ideology of hope from which a new black culture would spring, explains the emphasis that the Movement placed on the solidarity of the oppressed. Economic and political liberation, indeed black liberation itself, required black cultural hegemony. To paraphrase Gwyn Williams, Black Consciousness sought to create a social order in which the black way of life and thought would be dominant, a social order in which the black concept of reality would be diffused throughout society in all its institutional and private manifestations, informing with its spirit all taste, morality, customs, religious and political principles, and all social relations, particularly in their intellectual and moral connotation.[37]

This book will therefore explore the meaning and the content of black hegemony as described by Black Consciousness; it will suggest that the Movement was not merely an attempt at establishing a total cultural hegemony, but also a radical cry for the transformation of the structures which support white capitalism; it will show that the Movement was a situational philosophy of praxis and as such subject to modification, progression, and retrogression; and finally it will submit that the Movement entailed the necessary reaffirmation of the humanity of black people and the indispensable rediscovery of the rich history of Africa.

The hegemony of the white ruling class which instilled into the black mind a sense of inadequacy and inferiority had to be eliminated, and a new black identity had to be constructed to take its place. A general political crisis had to be engineered to contest the foundation of white supremacy and ultimately to strip it of its aura of legitimacy. In this context, the first phase of the revolutionary emancipation of black South Africans resided in the struggle for ideological hegemony; a struggle which had to erode the colonial mentality established by years of white domination and which had to usher in an entirely new system of beliefs. In a theoretical context, it is at this juncture that consciousness becomes a revolutionary force. In the words of Antonio Gramsci:

> Man is above all else mind, consciousness—that is, he is a product of history, not nature. There is no other way of explaining why socialism has not come into existence already, although there have always been exploiters and exploited, creators of wealth and selfish consumers of wealth. Man has only been able to acquire a sense of his worth bit by bit, in one sector of society after another . . . . And such awareness was not generated out of brute physiological needs, but out of intelligent reasoning, first of all by a few and later by entire social classes who perceived the causes of certain social facts and understood that there might be ways of converting the structure of repression into one of rebellion and social reconstruction. This means that every revolution has been preceded by an intense labour of social criticism, of cultural penetration and diffusion.[38]

Such an "intense labour of social criticism, of cultural penetration and diffusion" was precisely the task that the Black Consciousness Movement had set for itself. The next chapters are an analysis of its ideological and concrete manifestations.

Chapter III

The Growth and Definition of the Black Consciousness Movement

The repression unleashed by the white state in the early 1960's against the nationalist movements of African liberation created a political vacuum. The bannings of the African National Congress (ANC) and the Pan Africanist Congress (PAC) in 1960 left the African population without any viable means of protest and internal opposition. This absence of challenge to apartheid profoundly shaped the political development of the mid-1960's. It provoked the ascendancy of a small class of white liberals bent on defending what it perceived to be the interests of a defenseless African population. It induced an African political opportunism manifested in the rise of a Bantustan administrative elite. Finally, it permitted the consolidation of the repressive machinery of white supremacy.

Yet it was clear that neither white liberals nor Bantustan leaders obtained the support of the African masses. These masses were in fact more concerned about survival than about the niceties of an increasingly irrelevant white liberalism, or the false promises of Bantustan development. Their fight for survival was not only an indication of the masses' existential misery; it was also part of a larger malady of fear, demoralization, and submissiveness. It was in this context of despair that the first seeds of Black Consciousness began to take root and grow.

Not surprisingly, these first seeds were planted by African students. As Martin Legassick has argued: ". . . students who are the highly educated few of an oppressed class, group or nation have often claimed, especially if their own avenues for social advancement are blocked, that to be an intellectual is to be a revolutionary."[1] Yet it is ironical that this generation of black youth, the first to be educated in the "virtues" of apartheid at the "tribal colleges,"[2] freed itself from white hegemony to develop the most systematic ideological challenge to apartheid itself. Be that as it may, in the mid-1960's the black students were probably the only black social group to have escaped from the prevalent mood of despair.

Black students have always been obsessed with liberation, and they have always been the vanguard of African resistance. As members of the National Union of South African Students (NUSAS)—although it was banned on black campuses—black students were part of one of the few remaining legal organizations opposed to apartheid. Yet, precisely because legality required liberal-based, meliorist policies, NUSAS could no longer satisfy the increasingly radical demands of black students. Moreover, as Legassick and Shingler remarked:

> . . . [NUSAS' leaders were faced with a unique dilemma which] reflected their position as white critics of white supremacy. As whites, they were inextricably part of the very system they criticized. In effect, to support the goals of NUSAS was to support, at least by implication, the demise of a political and social structure that secured them their status and within which they operated, and to promote, at least indirectly, changes that might end by inflicting loss and suffering, perhaps indiscriminately, on the white community. And yet, because they were not committed to action commensurate with their goals . . . they were open to charges by non-whites of hypocrisy, timidity, and squeamishness, and even of objective support of the existing system.[3]

Furthermore, blacks considered themselves at best as aliens within the white dominated NUSAS and at worst as token emblems of NUSAS' sanctimonious multiracialism:

> Despite its multiracial membership, NUSAS was essentially white-populated, white-financed, white-led and white-controlled, although its policies ran counter to the nationally dominant white consensus. Non-whites, as delegates and office-holders, did play a role, but were for the most part overshadowed by their white counterparts, and in some instances were callously used and manipulated as symbols of NUSAS' integrated nonracialism.[4]

These dilemmas which faced NUSAS were to be shared—albeit in varying degrees—by other multiracial organizations opposed to apartheid. Among those, the University Christian Movement (UCM) formed in 1966 emerged as a voice of Christian witness against white supremacy. For black students UCM became an alternative to NUSAS' remoteness and liberal meliorism. It facilitated a renewal of dialogue amongst them and provided the first forum for the Black Consciousness Movement. Barney Pityana, who was to become one of the central figures of the Movement and the South African Students' Organization (SASO), wrote:

> The establishment of the University Movement (UCM) . . . opened new avenues for contact. UCM had a special appeal to students at the University Colleges. The fact that within a year and a half of its existence UCM had already a black majority in its sessions is indicative of this. Hence with the continued getting together of students from the University Colleges, dialogue began again amongst black students.[5]

The ultimate outcome of this dialogue was a severe blow to multiracialism, and UCM itself became the target of criticism.[6] Ranwedzi Nengwekhulu, who emerged as the full time organizer of SASO, revealed the prevalent feelings of the Movement:

> Concern was expressed that such organization as NUSAS and the University Christian Movement were white-dominated and, as such, paid very little attention to problems pertaining to the Black students

community. In fact, some people began to doubt the very com-
petence of a pluralistic group, especially where the unaffected group
is from the oppressor camp. It was felt that a time had come when
Blacks had to formulate their own thinking unpolluted by ideas
emanating from a group with a good deal at stake in the status
quo.[7]

Blacks began to assert that their future lay in their own black
hands. Hence, a great part of the impetus for the Black Consciousness Movement originated in the inadequacies of a multiracialism distorted by the weight of white hegemony.

Amongst blacks the conviction spread that whites' interests
and aspirations were no longer identical to theirs, but were in
fact antagonistic. This statement was not new; it first developed
in the Lembede wing of the ANC's Youth League during the
late 1940's and 1950's, and it culminated in the formation of
the PAC in 1959.[8] Yet, what differentiated the Black Consciousness Movement from Lembedism or Africanism was its
originality in elaborating an ideology of hope rooted in the
theology of liberation; this in turn led to an emphasis on the
solidarity of the oppressed irrespective of their race.

While Africanists paid lip service to the idea of an "African
National Church" and identified with the "independent churches"
of the "Ethiopian" and "Zionist" types,[9] they never developed
an alternative theology to the dominant bourgeois cultic ethos.[10]
Engulfed in an anti-white feeling which reflected their rejection
of white church leadership and resentment at white society for
downgrading their own African interpretation of Christianity,
the independent churches insisted on an essentially God-given
salvation. Alternatively they developed an eccentric messianism
which found ultimate expression in a belief that Africans were
immune to the white man's bullets.[11] Thus, while it is true that
their version of Christianity stressed the deprivation, exploitation, and misery of the Africans, it never seriously challenged
the hegemony of bourgeois Christian ideology.

This is precisely where the Black Consciousness Movement
began; for the ideology it developed rejected the status quo to
produce a new Christian paradigm bent on revolutionizing both

the material structure and cultural superstructure of South Africa. Indeed, in opposition to the Africanists' search for an exclusively African culture, the Black Consciousness Movement sought to develop a culture of the oppressed as a means of transforming the whole of society into a new and superior ethical order.

This is not to say that the Movement devalued the African heritage, but rather that it integrated it into a wider intellectual construct and made it a vital component of a culture of human liberation. This culture of human liberation formed a complex and multifaceted world-view dominated only in the last instance by its African specificity. The Movement therefore embraced not only Africans and their superstructure, but also those groups suffering from comparable exploitation.[12] The emancipation of the Africans involved the emancipation of the oppressed as a whole. As such, Black Consciousness was a part of a universal consciousness determined to transform the world.

By the end of the 1960's a new generation of black youth began to articulate the necessity of an intellectual and psychological liberation from white-bourgeois hegemony. Blacks had reached a stage of crisis by discovering a series of existential anomalies which deviated from the expectations generated by white liberal discourse. The existential anomalies had reached such massive and egregious proportions that blacks abandoned liberalism altogether. It was in this context that the Black Consciousness Movement was born.

In December 1968, at Marianhill, black students formed the South African Students' Organization (SASO) which was officially inaugurated in July 1969 at Turfloop—the tribal University College of the North. It is important to note that at this stage SASO adopted a limited student concern, a "student-as-such"[13] position, and continued to use the term "non-white" to define its ethnic character.[14] Initially SASO still considered NUSAS as the national union of South African students, so placing itself in a defensive corner.

Indeed, at first SASO leaders felt compelled to justify their very existence as an exclusively non-white organization. Would they not be acquiescing in the structures of apartheid if they rejected the multiracial forum of NUSAS? Would they not become black racists? But as Steve Biko—SASO's first President and the major figure of the Black Consciousness Movement—explained, considerable uneasiness created a shift in student attitudes:

> Not only was the move (the formation of SASO) taken by the non-white students defensible but it was a long overdue step. It seems sometimes that it is a crime for the non-white students to think for themselves. The idea of everything being done for the blacks is an old one and all liberals take pride in it; but once the black students want to do things for themselves suddenly they are regarded as becoming 'militant'. . . . The fact that the whole ideology centers around non-white students as a group might make a few people to believe that the organization (SASO) is racially inclined. Yet what SASO has done is simply to take stock on the present scene in the country and to realize that not unless the non-white students decide to lift themselves from the doldrums will they ever hope to get out of them. What we want is not black visibility but real black participation. In other words it does not help us to see several quiet black faces in a multiracial student gathering which ultimately concentrates on what the white students believe are the needs for the black students.[15]

However, the fact that SASO felt compelled to explain at length its break from "multiracialism" indicated that it had not fully freed itself from white liberal hegemony. SASO had rejected white liberal ideology, but it had not yet developed its own ethico-political understanding of history.

A new black analysis was soon initiated. In 1970, SASO abandoned its limited student position and extended its intellectual message well beyond the confines of the tribal campuses. The problem was not simply being members of a discriminated against black community; as Pityana argued, it was above all belonging to an alienated oppressed social group:

> Black students owe their first allegiance to the black community with whom they share the burdens and injustices of apartheid. . . .
> It is essential for the black students to strive to elevate the level of consciousness of the black community by promoting awareness, pride, achievement and capabilities. In the long run this will prove

far more valuable than the sentimental and idealistic attitude of perpetually trying to "bridge the gap" between races.[16]

Moreover, a new aggressiveness replaced the earlier defensiveness, as SASO moved into an offensive role. This crystalized as SASO withdrew its recognition of NUSAS: it was not a true national union. The argument was as follows:

> There is a dichotomy between principle and practice in the organization. We reject their basis of integration as being based on standards predominantly set by white society. It is more of what the white man expects the black man to do than the other way around. We feel we do not have to prove ourselves to anybody. . . . All in all SASO feels NUSAS is a National Union on paper only, while in practice it is essentially a white English students' organization.[17]

There was no longer a need to justify the black break from NUSAS, not only because the sentiments of the white liberal establishment became irrelevant to the black struggle, but also because multiracialism within apartheid society represented trickery and untruth. SASO contended that:

> The student population *is* already divided into laagers, and the so called "open" organizations represented a farcical non-racial front that enjoys little support from all quarters and often is a cause for bitter strifes within the black student ranks. It might be more effective to go it alone instead of standing piously on ineffective platforms, issuing impotent fulminations against the "system."[18]

If in 1970 SASO rejected white liberal multiracialism without apology, it had merely outlined in vague and confused sketches its new ethico-political concepts. A year later, however, the rupture with white liberalism materialized in a radically independent philosophy of history which contained four inseparable elements:

(1) The formation of an ethico-political ideology capable of liberating the blacks from their own mental submissiveness to white cultural hegemony.

(2) A radical critique of the pretensions and aims of white liberalism.

(3) The solidarity of the black people as a means to ending their existential misery.

(4) The definition of black as a socially exploited group of people.

The SASO policy manifesto adopted in 1971 formulated these new conceptions and became the single most important document of the Black Consciousness Movement, a document which was continuously enriched by further intellectual reflection and by the coming struggles for black emancipation.

> SASO is a Black Student Organization working for the liberation of the Black man first from psychological oppression by themselves through inferiority complex and secondly from physical oppression occurring out of living in a White racist society.
>
> We define Black people as those who are by law or tradition, politically, economically and socially discriminated against as a group in the South African society and identifying themselves as a unit in the struggle towards the realization of their aspirations.
>
> SASO believes: . . . That . . . because of the privileges accorded to them by legislation and because of their continual maintenance of an oppressive regime Whites have defined themselves as part of the problem. . . . That in all matters relating to the struggle towards realizing our aspirations, Whites must be excluded. . . . That this attitude not be interpreted by Blacks to imply "anti-Whitism" but merely a more positive way of attaining a normal situation in South Africa.
>
> . . . SASO upholds the concept of Black Consciousness and the drive towards Black awareness as the most logical and significant means of ridding ourselves of the shackles that bind us to perpetual servitude.
>
> . . . SASO accepts the premise that before the Black people should join the open society, they should first close their ranks, to form themselves into a solid group to oppose the definite racism that is meted out by the White society, to work out their direction clearly and bargain from a position of strength. SASO believes that a truly open society can only be achieved by Blacks.
>
> SASO believes that the concept of integration can never be realized in an atmosphere of suspicion and mistrust. Integration does not mean an assimilation of Blacks into an already established set of norms drawn up and motivated by White society. Integration implies free participation by individuals in a given society and proportionate contribution to the joint culture of the society by all constituent

groups. . . . Integration follows automatically when the doors to prejudice are closed through the attainment of a just and free society.

SASO believes that all groups allegedly working for "Integration" in South Africa . . . and here we note in particular the Progressive Party and other liberal institutions . . . are not working for the kind of integration that would be acceptable to the Black man. Their attempts are directed merely at relaxing certain oppressive legislations and to allow Blacks into a White-type society.[19]

The Black Consciousness Movement represented the unifying thread of black resistance in the 1970's, and it will continue to influence—albeit in new forms—future black revolutionaries. While the Movement initially represented a diffuse tendency rather than a neatly consistent ideology, it gradually developed a clear and consistent theoretical core. This, however, did not necessarily indicate complete analytical agreement between all advocates of Black Consciousness. Manifesting an aversion to any closed philosophical systems, the Movement was essentially an open-ended articulation of the blacks' existential situation. As such, the material conditions of livelihood had a serious and direct impact on the elaborations of the diverse streams of Black Consciousness.

For black petty bourgeois of the Bantustans and the urban centers, the Movement was merely a mental construct which allowed them to challenge white supremacy on a purely cultural sphere. The petty bourgeoisie could thus escape—in its imagination—from the stigmas of its color by asserting its equality and even the superiority of black to white civilization. Hence, Black Consciousness for this class was a way out of an impossible situation; it detracted it from its color-based, inferior status by restoring its self-denied blackness.

This is why it was beyond the capacity of petty bourgeois Black Consciousness to supersede the classical motto "Black is beautiful," which it discovered to be the "slogan of the times."[20] Indeed, petty bourgeois adopted the Movement only insofar as it offered to reestablish their humanity as black people within the existing structures of the economy; they stopped short of developing an ideology transcending the capitalist order. The goal was not revolutionizing society, but institutionalizing the equal participation of capitalists of all color in the economic system.

It is no wonder that the president of the National African Federated Chambers of Commerce, Mr. Motsuenyane, outlined the tasks remaining for black liberation in the true spirit of capitalism:

> The Black entrepreneur operates within a restricted and restrictive milieu. His scope is limited and oriented towards meeting only the needs of his own community, instead of the needs of the country and its people as a whole. He is debarred from establishing big competitive Company retail operations in the Urban industrial areas of South Africa. . . .
>
> The economy of this country, which is White-dominated at the top, will have to change and be restructured in such a manner as to offer the Black people a large measure of participation as full partners in all spheres of our commercial and industrial life.
>
> In order to make this major policy adjustment possible, the Black man must come to be regarded as a full citizen of this country, entitled to all benefits and privileges enjoyed by every South African regardless of his colour. The artificial impediments which deny him the right of forming companies, and establishing large business enterprises in Urban areas, should be nullified. . . . The Black man's task will be to demand a new role in the National economy of South Africa. . . . He should become an entrepreneur in his own right and a contributor to the overall economic growth of the country.[21]

From these remarks it becomes clear that the black petty-bourgeoisie was not prepared to relinquish the material and political advantages accruing from its association with white capitalism. Indeed, black liberation meant the further integration of blacks into the modified structure of a capitalist economy devoid of color; Black Consciousness in this instance was the spirit of black capitalism, a matter of material expediency and ideological accommodation rather than an ethico-political rupture.

To discover such ethico-political rupture, one must turn to the Black Consciousness Movement as it developed in SASO and in other black organizations—in particular the Black Peoples Convention (BPC) formed in 1971 and the Black Community

Program (BCP). Within these realms, the consciousness of being black was more than a matter of color. It represented the existential misery of oppressed social groups of diverse ethnies which had discovered that the source of their deprivations was not pre-ordained or theocentric, but anthropocentric. The awareness of the anthropocentric had an enormous impact on the Movement. Since oppression was the outcome of conscious human activities, further human action could result in the demise of oppression.

The awareness of the anthropocentric was limited to a select number of blacks, because as a group, black people had accepted their subjugated fate, not only because of an ever present repression, but above all because they identified themselves as less than human. White hegemony had in effect rendered blackness synonymous with evil, backwardness, and even nothingness. Blackness was a pathetic nihilism. In these conditions, the only escape was a denial of blackness and an alienated appropriation of whiteness. In the words of Adam Small, a black poet and intellectual exponent of the Movement:

> Whites have for so long been dominant in South Africa—and in other parts of the world—that it is difficult for us who have partly come to recognize that indeed we are not white, to get those fellow-men of ours who also are indeed not white, but who have not yet recognized the facts to share this recognition with us. The reason why they have not yet come to this recognition that they are not white is that they still look upon White as an equivalent concept with Value. This is what the dominance of whites has done to the psychology of those fellowmen of ours. It has sapped their will and made them sluggish and indeed unwilling to draw themselves away from Valuableness. Their equation of Whiteness with Valuableness is foolish and indeed dangerous for them, as it will destroy them.[22]

The blacks' fascination with whiteness was also the product of a systematic destruction of black history. The maintenance of white supremacy required the negation of past African civilizations. The acceptance of the existence of past African civilizations would have meant that blacks were indeed homofabers and as such capable of maintaining and transforming diverse conceptions of the world. And since the framework of values sustaining white supremacy required the de-humanization of the black people, the remedy was the comprehensive sweeping of black history. Accordingly, the blacks were made to adopt the overall white perspective that African history began only with the arrival of the Caucasians. As Biko recognized:

> . . . in an effort to destroy completely the structures that had been built up in the African Society and to impose their imperialism with an unnerving totality the colonialists were not satisfied merely with holding a people in their grip and emptying the Native's brain of all form and content, they turned to the past of the oppressed people and distorted, disfigured and destroyed it. No longer was reference made to African culture, it became barbarism. . . .
>
> No doubt, therefore, part of the approach envisaged in bringing about "black consciousness" has to be directed to the past, to seek to rewrite the history of the black man and to produce in it the heroes who form the core of the African background. . . .[23]

While this rewriting of African history was not to be an uncritical approval of past traditions, it was to be an inspiration for transforming the present and shaping the just society of tomorrow. As the theologian Manas Buthelezi explained, there exists a:

> . . . tendency to romanticize the ethnographically reconstructed historical past at the expense of the anthropological dynamics of the present situation. To be sure, the past can serve as an important instrument for inspiring man in his present-day responsibilities . . . [yet] we should not forget that there is a difference between psychologically living in the past in order to escape from the harsh realities of the present which one cannot face squarely at the moment, and living in the past because it can give the spiritual and physical bread for the day.[24]

Hence, the African past, however glorious it may have been, should not impose itself as a monolithic conception of the world. The Black Consciousness Movement realized that the uncritical advocacy of the African past as the means towards the liberation of the oppressed in the twentieth century represented an unrealistic nationalist antidote. From this perspective can be understood Njabulo Ndebele's attack on the static stream of African tradition:

> . . . customs and traditions are man-made, therefore they can be changed according to whether man continues to find value in them. No sooner has man created something than he either wants to improve on what he has made or create something else. Culture therefore is essentially dynamic. That is why the blacks must set about destroying the old and static customs and traditions that have over the past decades made Africa the world's human zoo and museum of human evolution.[25]

This should not be construed as an attack on black traditions as such; rather it represented a search for an ideological break from a superseded and yet respected heritage. This ideological break had at its roots the concept of blackness, and it relied to a considerable extent on the importation of black American thoughts and ideas. Indeed, the intellectual manifestations of the American Black Power Movement, expressed in the writings of Stokeley Carmichael, Charles Hamilton, Eldridge Cleaver, Malcom X, James Cone, and others, generated amongst black South Africans a clearer interpretation of their own existential conditions.[26]

However, it would be wrong to exaggerate the black American contribution to the Black Consciousness Movement. What the American Black Power ideology provided was a theoretical source for the renewal of black South African thinking. It accelerated the development of the Movement helping to transform existential feelings into ethico-political conceptions of the world. The black South African intelligentsia discovered in Black Power ideology the basis for generating a new theoretical paradigm, but one which had to be adapted and reconciled with its own peculiar social conditions.

The United States was not South Africa, and the liberation of the black people in America could not be equated with that of the black South Africans. This was made clear by Biko during his testimony at the trial of nine of his comrades.[27] In response to the contention that Black Power was identical to Black Consciousness, Biko declared:

> Well, they certainly are not. I think the end result of the goal of
> Black Power is fundamentally different from the goal of Black
> consciousness in this country. . . . Black Power is the preparation
> of a group for participation in already established society, and Black
> Power therefore in the States operates like a minority philosophy.
> . . .[28]

Hence, while black power in the United States was a minority philosophy, the Black Consciousness Movement sought to encompass the totality of South Africa. In short, in South Africa, the goal of the Movement was the ultimate hegemony of blackness as an ethico-political conception of liberation. As Biko recognized, the issue was not integration in the existing white-dominated system, but rather to revolutionize the system into a black creation:

> Blacks no longer seek to reform the system because so doing
> implies acceptance of the major points around which the system
> revolves.
> Blacks are out to completely transform the system and to make
> of it what they wish. Such a major undertaking can only be realized
> in an atmosphere where people are convinced of the truth inherent
> in their stand. Liberation therefore, is of paramount importance in
> the concept of Black consciousness, for we cannot be conscious of
> ourselves and yet remain in bondage.[29]

Thus, Black Consciousness became a revolutionary theory. Its immediate task was to make possible this complete transformation of the white system and this liberation of the black people. The problems involved in this restructuring of society as a whole were immensely complex, requiring much more than the mere negation of the negativities created by institutionalized racism. Black Consciousness was in fact the antithetical stage in the long and difficult process of dialectical liberation. As such it contradicted the thesis—white racism—and yet, it remained conditioned by white racism itself. This is why Bennie Khoapa understood the Movement as a series of "transcendent negations":

> Paradoxically, a prerequisite for human solidarity is a feeling of
> non-solidarity with men who stand in the way of solidarity. Par-

adoxically, the oppressed can only bring about a future of universal brotherhood in proportion as they feel and exhibit group solidarity with the enemies of human solidarity. . . . History has charged us with the cruel responsibility of going to the very gate of racism in order to destroy racism—to the gate not further.[30]

As the antithetical stage of the revolutionary dialectic, the Black Consciousness Movement was bound to work for its own abolition. Indeed, it must be construed as an ethico-political philosophy of praxis whose ultimate end was its own annulment through the achievement of the task it had set out to accomplish. Once black people have engaged in revolutionary activity and erected the foundations of the new society, the Black Consciousness Movement will be superseded since the clash between the polar opposites will have resulted in a new synthesis.

In this sense, while the Black Consciousness Movement, as the antithetical stage of the dialectical negation of white racism represented the moving and creative principle, it could not become the conceptual philosophy of the synthesis. This conceptual philosophy of the synthesis was, to use Biko's term, a "true humanity" which could not be truly understood or created from the midst of a racist and capitalist society. A full understanding of it could only come from the midst of a classless and nonracist society. Thus, a true humanity in the Black Consciousness scheme was the revolutionary and dialectical actualization of a color-blind and classless society.

This implies that the positive vision of a true humanity envisaged by the Movement was a vague concept. If it represented a coherent and valuable critique of white bourgeois racism, it offered few indications of the just society of the future. However, this was not a proof of failure or inconsistency; it was rather the consequence of the revolutionary content of Black Consciousness.

Any theory which has as its goal the radical transformation of the existing historical reality can only offer a vague description of the new and revolutionized society. This is true because a new and revolutionized society is the product of a praxis which transforms not only the protagonists and their world-views, but also, and most importantly the very relations of production. The vision of a new order from the midst of the old order is inevitably deformed because the consciousness of the revolutionary class itself is still stamped with the intellectual and material limitations of the old order. It is only through the praxis of revolution that the new order can truly be grasped.

Thus, given the nature of the phenomenon Black Consciousness purported to explain, the lack of a programmatic vision of the future was a necessary occupational hazard. Furthermore, the Black Consciousness Movement did not offer a theory of the future. Its task was not to describe the classless society of tomorrow, but to ruthlessly criticize the existing white racist order in all its institutional manifestations with the hope of contributing to the rise of black hegemony, and black dignity. Biko's definition of Black Consciousness recognized this:

> Black Consciousness is an attitude of mind and a way of life.
> . . . Its essence is the realization by the black man of the need to
> rally together with his brothers around the cause of their oppres-
> sion—the blackness of their skin—and to operate as a group to rid
> themselves of the shackles that bind them to perpetual servitude.
> It is based on a self-examination which has ultimately led them to
> believe that by seeking to run away from themselves and emulate
> the white man, they are insulting the intelligence of whoever created
> them black. This philosophy of Black Consciousness therefore ex-
> presses group pride and the determination of the black to rise and
> attain the envisaged self. . . . On his own . . . the black man
> wishes to explore his surroundings and test his possibilities—in
> other words to make his freedom real by whatever means he deems
> fit. At the heart of this kind of thinking is the realization by blacks
> that the most potent weapon in the hands of the oppressor is the
> mind of the oppressed.[31]

From Biko's perspective then, Black Consciousness and black morality meant the realization of an understanding that the emancipation of blacks and the liberation of society as a whole required the mental renaissance of the black intellect. This understanding also meant the development of a black political will which, if necessary, would generate a massive insurrection culminating in the overthrow of white supremacy and the ushering in of black hegemony.

In its quest for liberation Black Consciousness rejected white liberalism and it envisaged the free society of the future in terms of its socialist transformation as well as its moral emancipation. Structural and material changes would not suffice; they would need to be supplemented by an intellectual and cultural revolution. As Biko put it:

> The liberals, Alan Paton and so on, one would reject at any stage, any stage be it now on up to the revolution. There are some white leftists who have attachment to, say, the same rough principles of post revolutionary society [as ourselves] but a lot of them are terribly cynical about for instance, the importance of the value systems which we enunciate so often, from the black consciousness angle. That it is not only capitalism that is involved; it is also the whole gamut of white value systems which has been adopted as standard by South Africa, both whites and blacks so far. . . . So your problems are not solved completely when you alter the economic pattern, to a socialist pattern. You still don't become what you ought to be.[32]

In this sense, the role of the Black Consciousness Movement was to liberate blacks from both their enslavement to white values and from their existential misery. To paraphrase Marx, Black Consciousness only showed the blacks what they were fighting for, and Black Consciousness was something that the blacks had to acquire, like it or not. The Movement, then, consisted only in enabling the blacks to clarify their consciousness, in waking them from their dream about themselves, in explaining to them the meaning of their own actions.[33] Hence, it was only when blacks understood their alienated and exploited condition that they would take upon themselves the responsibility of transforming their historical reality.

This is why it was so important that the Movement be "spread to reach all sections of the Black community,"[34] for to spread Black Consciousness was to break through the fog of white bourgeois hegemony. To perform this task SASO developed a strong following among African, Indian, and "Coloured" students. Its internal organization as well as its means of communications were highly effective. While it is difficult to assess its total membership, SASO claimed 4,000 subscribers to its regularly published newsletters. Moreover, SASO organized many well-attended conferences where the Black Consciousness ideology was discussed and proselytized. In any event it is safe to accept Gail Gerhart's conclusion that SASO raised the emerging black intelligentsia to a "level of political education and ideological diffusion never before achieved by any black political organization."[35]

In this sense, the Movement eroded and ultimately displaced the hegemony of white bourgeois culture. It created a new ethos rooted in a new system of black values. As the SASO policy manifesto contended:

> The basic tenet of Black consciousness is that the Blackman must reject all value systems that seek to make him a foreigner in the country of his birth and reduce his basic human dignity.
> The Blackman must build up his own value systems, see himself as self-defined and not as defined by others.[36]

Hence SASO's slogan: "Black man, you are on your own."

To be on your own, however, implied neither the growth of a black possessive individualism, nor a total retrenchment into blackness. On the contrary, to be on your own was to be part of an oppressed group determined to transform its existential conditions as a group. It was from this concept of an oppressed group that the Black Consciousness Movement developed a sophisticated analysis of social classes and in so doing became much more than the cultural manifestation of a frustrated petty bourgeois black intelligentsia.

Chapter IV

Class, Blackness, and Economics

Because its primary interest lay in the analysis of the superstructure of South African society, the Black Consciousness
Movement was always in danger of jettisoning an understanding
of the material forces of society. By stressing the importance
of culture, Black Consciousness tended to reduce the emancipation of black people to a process of psychological and intellectual renaissance. Yet, the fragmentation of the black population into different groups entertaining different visions of the
future contributed to a subtle change in the Black Consciousness
Movement's locus of interest. As the fragmentation of the black
population became more obvious, Black Consciousness struggled
more intensely to comprehend this reality.

The discovery of class and economics as intellectual tools for
black liberation stemmed not from a careful reading of Marx
or Engels or Mao, but rather from the social divisions which

81

plagued black unity. Although Black Consciousness was indebted to the African socialist thinkers such as Nkrumah, Nyerere, Fanon, Machel, Cabral and others, its radicalization was essentially due to the existential realities of South Africa.

The socio-political developments which were occurring in the newly independent African states also influenced the Movement, confirming the insights generated in South Africa itself. The fundamental lesson was that political independence and Africanization of the existing state bureaucracy were necessary but wholly insufficient steps in the long march toward black emancipation. The intellectuals of the Black Consciousness Movement clearly saw that independence without fundamental structural changes was at best a first stage toward these transformations; at worst it was a mystification whereby the black bourgeoisie, in alliance with imperialism, joined in the systematic exploitation of the African masses.

This implied that in South Africa the enemy was not merely whites as an ethnically homogenous group of exploiters. The enemy was also the "non-whites," the group of elitist blacks aspiring vainly to the privileges of whiteness in the established economic system. In structural terms, the Movement recognized that racism and apartheid were nurtured and sustained by capitalism, and that therefore the liberation of the black people required the abolition of capitalism itself. With this understanding, Black Consciousness began to change the emphasis of its analysis from an essentially cultural and racial explanation of black misery and alienation to class conflicts and economics. The focus was now the overall impact of capitalism and imperialism on the cultural, social, and material conditions of black people.

It is difficult to say precisely when this change occurred, but it appears that the historical conjuncture of the early and mid-1970's, both within and without South Africa, precipitated it. There was the Sono affair and the student revolts of 1972,[1] the Durban strikes of 1973, the beginnings of massive repression against Black Consciousness' advocates in 1974 and the coming independence of the Transkei. The Tanzanian experiment, the collapse of the Portuguese empire and the rise to power of black socialist-marxist regimes in Mozambique, Angola and Guinea-Bissau contributed also to the radicalization of Black Consciousness.

It is important to emphasize that this radicalization of Black Consciousness meant neither an uncritical espousal of class analysis, nor a rejection of the ethnic theory of oppression. Blackness remained central to the analysis, but to it was added a materialistic conception of history purporting to explain the unity of the white ethnie, and the fragmentation of the black bloc. Because color determined the privileged position of the white ethnie the possibility of a proletarian alliance between black and white workers was nil. The behavior of whites as a whole was dictated by their color and not by their class. To put it another way, to be white was to be acculturated into the bourgeoisie and consequently the white proletarian consciousness was stultified. In Bennie Khoapa's terms:

> There is a growing belief that in the classical sense white workers cannot be regarded as genuine workers as long as they hide behind job reservation, discriminatory wages, discriminatory recognition of their trade unions and the general pool of privileges open to whites in South Africa.[2]

Hence, a serious tension existed between class theory and the reality of the color-bar; race transcended class and polarized the different ethnies in bitter antagonism. Apartheid society, it was argued, had deep racist roots which could not simply be understood as a class problem. The racial subordination of Africans complicated an already complex set of class relationships and shattered the hopes of a color-blind consciousness. As Barney Pityana explained:

> A class is formed when persons who perform the same function in the production process become aware of their common interests and unite to promote them against the opposing class. Thus in order that a group of people can bring about change there must be an identity of interests which they seek to protect and promote. I submit that any identity of interest between Black and White is effectively stifled by the colour conflict.[3]

This was the basis of the Black Consciousness Movement's analysis of the white bloc which was held responsible for racism and white supremacy. The few whites who had joined the blacks in their struggle could not justify the absolution of the white bloc as a whole. All whites were guilty, whether or not they actively participated in the crimes perpetuated against the black race. No wonder then, that Karl Jaspers' description of "metaphysical guilt" was approvingly quoted by Biko:

> There exists among men, because they are men, a solidarity through which each shares responsibility for every injustice and every wrong committed in the world, and especially for crimes that are committed in his presence or of which he cannot be ignorant. If I do not do whatever I can to prevent them, I am an accomplice in them.[4]

Thus, it was only by total identification with the suffering of the blacks, and indeed only by a willingness to die on their side that a white person could truly experience being black. Short of this commitment, the ambivalence of white liberals and philanthropists was intolerable and condemned.

At the root of this sentiment was the judgment that white liberals were responsible for arresting the black revolutionary élan and for filling the black intellectual mind with the mythical vision of non-racialism. In the words of Nengwekhulu:

> . . . white liberals have indeed been criminally responsible for arresting and aborting the struggle by playing the role of a bulwark, a kind of buffer zone between the blacks and the White system which has been oppressing us for centuries. In fact, to us, the white liberal establishment's involvement in the Black struggle is its desire to kill the revolutionary zeal of the Black masses by promising them a "controlled" change which will result in some mythical, "mosaic" multi-racialism.[5]

Moreover, as Biko pointed out,

> . . . in adopting the line of a non-racial approach, the liberals are playing their old game. They are claiming a "monopoly on intelligence and moral judgement" and setting the pattern and pace for

the realization of the black man's aspirations. They want to remain in good books with both the black and white worlds. They want to shy away from all forms of "extremism," condemning "white supremacy" as being just as bad as "Black Power!" . . . The myth of integration as propounded under the banner of liberal ideology must be cracked and killed because it makes people believe that something is being done when in actual fact the artificial integrated circles are soporific on the blacks and provide a vague satisfaction for the guilty-stricken whites.[6]

The one vital lesson which the Black Consciousness Movement had learned was that the goal of racial integration would be futile, and even suicidal, if it respected the cultural, economic, and moral norms of white liberalism. A meaningful integration could not be separated and excluded from the overall transformation of the existing white racist capitalism. This radical conception of integration in a context of economic transformation was clearly stated by Khoapa:

Men do not and cannot love each other if their material interests conflict. As long as institutions, particularly economic institutions, make it necessary for one group to hate another in order to maximize its position, then integration is impossible . . . Racial integration requires economic integration, and this in turn, requires a recognition that the race problem cannot be solved without profound structural modifications in the country; . . . racial problems can only be solved in a climate of economic equality.[7]

Thus, integration, in white liberal terms meant a pseudo-integration which prevented blacks from thinking adequately about themselves and about their material conditions. It meant also the creation of a deformed culture—deformed in the sense that it was not the result of a common experience but the imposition of an exclusively white liberal paradigm. As Biko observed,

If by integration you understand a break-through into white society by blacks, an assimilation and acceptance of blacks into an already established set of norms and code of behaviour set up by and maintained by whites, then YES I am against it. . . . If on the other hand by integration you mean there shall be free participation by all members of a society, catering for the full expression of the self in a freely changing society as determined by the will of the people, then I am with you. For one cannot escape the fact that the culture shared by the majority group in any given society must ultimately determine the broad direction taken by the joint culture of that society.[8]

Biko's claim that the culture of the majority was to establish itself as the hegemonic element of the joint culture was the ultimate condemnation of the white liberal way of life. The Black Consciousness Movement rejected liberalism not only because it embodied the white experience, but above all because it represented the individualism of bourgeois materialism. This bourgeois materialism worked like an acid on African culture, destroying its sense of purpose and its traditional communal outlook.

The Movement therefore recognized the gap between bourgeois material existence and the alienating emptiness of human relations in bourgeois society. It condemned the conditions of everyday life, the capitalistic-induced erosion of communal solidarity, and African corporate personality. The acquisitive obsession of bourgeois materialism was ravaging African culture and sapping its consensual foundations. Bonganjalo Goba had these biting words for bourgeois materialism and those blacks who embraced this possessive individualism:

In this country many of us black people have allowed ourselves to be victims of individualism and capitalism. We are no longer living as a dynamic community; we have lost so much of our sense of corporate personality. Influenced by capitalism we have become materialistically self-centered, and the emphasis seems to be on individual enterprise and material acquisition for the individual— not for the black masses. . . .[9]

While this position was in line with the traditional Africanist criticism of Western civilization, it was original in that although its reference was to the past, its aim was to revolutionize the present in order to create a better tomorrow:

To discover our rightful place in this country, we need a deeply rooted sense of solidarity, a sense of a dynamic, relevant black community. For this we need to rediscover the meaning of this concept with all its practical implications; we need to look back at what we have lost and re-examine our present strategies.[10]

The point here is that the Black Consciousness Movement could not afford the luxury of ignoring the solidarity of traditional African culture, because it was precisely through nurturing and reviving that solidarity that blacks could confront the white power structure. In other words when the Movement stressed its attachment to the African tradition, its aim was not the restoration of some idyllic past civilization, but rather the sophisticated use of that civilization for the furtherance of the contemporary black struggle. As Manas Buthelezi argued:

> The realization of our authentic humanity as black people does not consist merely in reconstructing the old patterns of a past theological and sociological world-view, but in gaining access as black people to that which constitutes the wholeness of life in the present day world. Whatever lasting spiritual insights the old world-view contained will be activated only as we realize our humanity by meaningfully sharing in all the life facilities the present day world offers.[11]

Thus, the relevance of the past, it was argued, stemmed from the revolutionary praxis of the present, for it was by making history that men and women became aware of the potentialities of otherwise dying traditions. By participating in the historical process the masses would contribute to its accelerated transformation. Old conceptions would be perceived in a new perspective as society would reveal itself as an incomplete achievement in need of radical social change.

This new critical perception would provoke the prise de conscience and usher in a period of hope—a period during which the oppressed would discover their humanity and their power not as isolated individuals but as members of an exploited class determined to confront the structures of exploitation. Such a transformation of consciousness was indicated by these challenging words of S.T.M. Magagula at the general SASO conference of 1973:

> If white power has dominated and exploited the black man for these centuries, it is only right and proper that another power should be evolved that would challenge it and bring the world to harmony and justice. That power is . . . BLACK POWER![12]

These words expressed the dominant attitude of the Movement. The idea was that black liberation could only be the result of a coalescence of blacks into a solid power bloc. The point was made in this way by Khoapa:

> This is a world of groups. A man's power depends ultimately on the power of his group. This means that oppressed individuals must recognize their common interests and create a group. Groupness is a simple exigency of the situation. The oppressed can only extricate themselves by a regroupement.[13]

The fundamental struggle at this point in South African history was not a class struggle but a racial struggle. The class struggle existed, but as a phenomenon within the bounds of the South African ethnies. In other words, the class struggle existed among blacks, and among whites, but it had not yet become interracial. Moreover, while the class struggle divided blacks to such an extent that it pushed a significant minority towards the economic privileges and bourgeois culture of whites, it never acquired such intensity in the white bloc—whites were never pushed towards blackness.

The class struggle not only fragmented black resistance and black regroupment by inducing the formation of a black petty bourgeoisie, it also enhanced the overall powers of white supremacy. In the words of Ndebele,

> The greatest conflict is that between the races. . . . The white race tries to minimize the conflict within and between its ethnic groups in order to maximize its efforts to dominate; it also tries to maximize the conflict within and between the ethnic groups of the oppressed black race in order to minimize the latter's resistance in the racial conflict.[14]

Thus, the South African power structure was seen as reinforcing the political unity of the white ethnie under the protection of an hegemonic state; simultaneously, the white regime encouraged the polarization of the contradictory class interests within the diverse black ethnies and occupational strata. This is why the struggle for black emancipation was judged to be a racial and class struggle. Indeed, the Movement never confused the victorious ending of the racial struggle with black liberation; rather black liberation meant the ultimate resolution of the more fundamental class struggle. This crucial point lies at the root of the ideological development and revolutionary character of Black Consciousness. It is therefore imperative to analyze the concept of class as understood by Black Consciousness.

At the Black Renaissance Convention organized in 1974, Foszia Fisher and Harold Nxasana presented a paper entitled "The Labour Situation in South Africa" which expressed the point of view of the radical wing of Black Consciousness on the class nature of the black ethnie. They argued that white supremacy was not simply the result of military conquest; it also depended on co-opting a black minority into the structure and superstructure of the white system. This co-optation permitted the systematic exploitation of black labor without the permanent use of force. In this sense, some blacks became auxiliaries of the white system and also participated in the exploitation of their fellow blacks. The black ethnie was therefore polarized into two groups—those who survived by selling their cheap labor power, i.e., the workers; and those functionaries who had succeeded by attaching themselves to white society.

It remained true, however, that both black workers and black functionaries were oppressed because of their color. Yet, because their livelihood depended on divergent material conditions, they experienced differently the condition of oppression and they developed conflicting interests. In the words of Fisher and Nxasana:

> . . . to play their part in keeping the system of exploitation going, the functionaries had to be trained in the rules of the system. . . . Because they were educated in the same way as the colonists, and came to share their culture, they experienced the situation of oppression essentially as *discrimination*. . . . The workers on the other hand, experience their situation of oppression as one of exploitation.

> Discrimination exists but it is not the central issue. . . . To be exploited means to have no control over how you work or over how the product of your labour is to be used. It means that your body can be used to produce wealth for other people.[15]

This essential distinction between discrimination and exploitation had profound implications for the Black Consciousness Movement. It meant that despite the importance of the racial struggle it was ultimately the class struggle, that would determine the future of black South Africa. The Movement was therefore aware of the consequences of African independence in tropical Africa, an independence based solely on ending discrimination:

> In Africa, many of the independence movements were started by, or most strongly supported by, black civil servants who found that they were confined to the bottom rungs of the civil service. Their struggle for independence was a struggle for the right to move to the top of the civil service, but the civil service continued to perform its function of ensuring that the system of exploitation functioned properly.[16]

Hence, race discrimination was not by itself the source of exploitation; on the contrary, its abolition might constitute the perfect device for concealing continued exploitation.

The end of racial discrimination could be hailed by false prophets as the ultimate goal of black liberation, but in fact, it was but a stage in the process of liberation. Above all Black Consciousness demanded the abolition of exploitation:

> An end to discrimination . . . might only mean that there would be equal competition between black and white for positions among the exploiters . . . the functionaries have an interest in the abolition of discrimination while the workers have an interest in the abolition of exploitation.[17]

The abolition of discrimination represented the rights of privilege in an unequal class-ridden society; it was the legitimation of inequality. Equality would be the exclusive result of the eradication of exploitation, a process inextricably linked to the struggle of trade unions for worker's power. Therefore, it was not any kind of trade unionism that could provide the objective bases for equality. Indeed, it had to be a trade unionism bent on empowering workers and on changing the social relations of production. The mere struggle for higher wages was thoroughly insufficient, though necessary. As Fisher and Nxasana put it:

> In fact higher wages is always a secondary goal. The main goal is human dignity. . . . The aim of trade unionism is to change the workers from being part of the machinery into being full participants in industry. . . . Higher wages are merely a by-product of human dignity.[18]

While recognizing the possibility of a "middle-class" solution to the South African problem, Black Consciousness was in general confident that the black petty bourgeoisie would commit 'suicide as a class' to be reborn as a revolutionary vanguard. This suicide would neither be voluntary nor altruistic. Instead, it would be induced by the intransigence of the white state and the resulting material and intellectual weaknesses of the black petty bourgeoisie as a class.

Because of the white state's reluctance to end discrimination, the black petty bourgeoisie faced severely limited opportunities and perhaps extinction as a class. It would therefore be compelled to become revolutionary, to supersede its own class horizon, and to join the workers' struggle. To quote Fisher and Nxasana once more:

> . . . it is likely that the colonists in South Africa are too blinded by their own propaganda to use [the] division of interest between black functionaries and the black workers in order to divide people successfully.
> What this means is that the functionaries cannot hope to act independently to end discrimination. They can only hope to end it through a policy which will also end exploitation. Of course, the other alternative will be to accept discrimination as the price to be paid for the relative privilege of being a functionary, and many functionaries will doubtless choose this course. But many will not. We believe that the growth of "Black Consciousness" among the

black middle classes indicates a growing awareness of the extent to
which they have up till now been used as functionaries to keep the
system running.[19]

However, this optimistic position regarding the revolutionary
potential of the black petty bourgeoisie was not shared by all
advocates of the Black Consciousness Movement. In many
writings, the middle class was portrayed as so attached to white
capitalism that it was no longer interested in revolution. Indeed,
the petty bourgeoisie was the enemy of the black revolution as
it forsook its blackness to become a non-white stratum. Its
collaboration with the white system condemned it to a perennial
state of compromise which conflicted with the radical aims of
the Movement.

Being no longer capable of representing itself as the vanguard
of the struggle for black emancipation, the petty bourgeoisie
had lost the support of the black masses. Indeed, because du-
plicity was its way of life, the black middle class found itself
in a similar existential condition to white liberals. The doctors,
businessmen, lawyers, journalists, and other professional people
were the "darlings of the white liberals." They had become
"obsessed with capitalist values. They [had] the shared characteristic of indulging in the exploitation of their own people."[20]

The problem of analyzing the middle class and predicting its
role was exacerbated by the policy of separate development.
For, if the middle class was counter-revolutionary its position
would be enhanced by the rise of the tribal administrative elites
of the Bantustans. It is for these tribal elites that the Movement
reserved its most virulent criticisms, their role being comparable
to that of the hated black plantation drivers in American slavery:

> The leadership that the drivers gave to the quarters reflected the
> contradictory nature of their loyalties, experience, and social po-
> sition. In certain essential respects they provided a valuable symbol
> and rallying point for the slaves, but their ultimate reliance upon
> white sanction destroyed much of the potential long-term advantage.
> To serve their people at all, as well as to look after their personal
> interests, the drivers had to win the confidence of the masters. They
> had to become agents of order and discipline in the fields and the
> quarters. Necessarily, they had to crack the whip and to enforce

not only those rules which the community as a whole required for
good order but also those which the masters required for their own
narrower purposes. . . . To this extent, every driver assumed the
role of accomodationist and became the master's man.[21]

These elites lacked the logic, insight, and courage that would
have made them leaders of the black revolution. They were
blinded by their material egoism and they hardly dared to
conceive the idea of black liberation, for this idea was the very
negation of their existential condition. Furthermore, since their
only social base of power—outside white support—resided in
the intensification of tribalism they actively contributed to the
fragmentation of black resistance. These points were made clearly
in several SASO editorials:

> It is the elitist class that is sowing seeds of confusion and division
> amongst our people. It is the elitist class, created by the very
> oppressor that has joined hands with the oppressor in suppressing
> the legitimate aspirations of the masses of the people and they
> collect crumbs from the master's table for this dirty work. The
> chiefs are now part and parcel of this class. This is why Pretoria
> is creating them by the dozen.[22]

Such a severe condemnation of the tribal elites was an example
of part of an incisive criticism of the whole policy of separate
development which in turn led to radical criticisms of the whole
capitalist system. The linkages between tribal elites, separate
development, and capitalist exploitation were identified in Black
Consciousness literature and thoroughly condemned:

> Let blacks take full notice of the fact that the Transkei and other
> homelands are there not for our benefit but to maintain the chains
> that bind us into perpetual servitude by keeping us divided and
> involving us in useless and meaningless political exercises so as to
> keep our eyes away from the pot from which the racial poison is
> being brewed. They are there to ensure that the blacks never attain
> what they aspire for—their liberation. They are there to maintain
> the capitalist system of this country by keeping [the black man]
> starving and ignorant so that he can continue being a tool in the
> white man's farm, mine or industry for the production of wealth
> for the exclusive benefit of the white imperialist.

It is because of these reasons that blacks have to take positive action against these institutions. Each time we participate in them we are aiding the oppressor and actually participating in the emasculation and exploitation of the black man.[23]

These criticisms went even further as Black Consciousness writers discovered that the capitalist system was not simply a national phenomenon but a flexible, world system of hierarchical exploitation. Capitalism, it was argued, created an imperialism which manifested itself in the dialectical generation of both wealth and poverty, both inextricably tied to one another. It was not a static system of exploitation, it had to adapt to certain historical events, i.e., the combined pressures of the working classes in imperialist nations and the demands for independence of colonial peoples. In the words of Z. Mothopeng,

This doubled pronged attack by the working class movement on the one hand and by the liberation movement on the other hand forced the governments of the capitalist countries to grant certain concessions which did not however, affect the basic nature of capitalism. [The granting of these concessions, however, depended] heavily on the exploitation of the material and human resources of the colonial territories.[24]

Given this analysis, it is no wonder that the Black Consciousness Movement opposed the foreign economic penetration of South Africa, and particularly the Bantustans. Foreign investments were seen as material contributions to the consolidation of white supremacy; they were also seen as a means through which the white regime obtained the tacit support of alien capitalists for its exploitative policies. The more foreign capital implanted itself in South Africa the more it increased its stake in the survival of the status quo. Despite liberal claims to the contrary, foreign capital did not contribute to the overall development of black South Africa; instead it enriched the white population and propped up a new black class of pseudo-capitalists.

Foreign investments, as they occurred within the existing imperialist framework, could not be expected to ameliorate the social conditions of the black masses. Such capital penetrated South Africa precisely because it was determined to exploit black cheap labor. As a SASO editorial pointed out,

> There will be no end to exploitation and underdevelopment within the framework of the imperialist system. Foreign investors extract as it is, more and more basic materials, minerals, primary and secondary products, cheap labour and social comfort out of this country. . . . The fringe benefits being received by the Black elite are there to make it servile to western capitalist irregularities.[25]

This investment assured the " 'perpetuation of the imperialist division of labour' [and it came] wrapped in a fog of hypocrisy and paternalism."[26]

If foreign investments and western capitalism, black petty bourgeois and white liberals could not liberate the blacks, where was hope to be found? For Black Consciousness, liberation would come from blacks who suffered exploitation and became aware of this existential situation. Liberation would come when blacks realized they were not born to live and die in misery, but that they were human beings capable of revolutionizing the world.

In the analysis of Ndebele, however, this critical and revolutionary consciousness was not easily aroused, particularly among the peasants:

> The peasants on the white farms have almost no political consciousness. Their day is rigidly scheduled according to some form of compulsory routine. They have accepted, either consciously or subconsciously, the fact that they are not working for their own betterment; rather, they are working for a white master who seems to have a right to benefit from their labours. They have no social security. . . . What, therefore, can the peasant do? Nothing. It is a fact that on their own, they cannot do much. They are weakened, as a group, by ignorance; by lack of political awareness; by immediate ethnic differences which to them are still the determinants of the basic conflicts in life. This peasant group is, indeed, a good example of a power-group that has no actual power.[27]

Nevertheless, the peasants' "potential power is immense indeed."[28]

If the peasants had not yet acquired the critical consciousness required for black liberation, which class could fill the gap? Migrant laborers fared a little better—they were vaguely aware of the 'conspiracy of the rich':

> These migrant labourers suddenly find themselves uprooted from a rural life which they find uninspiring when compared with the stories of a glamorous life in the big cities. They come to the town and frequently mix with the urban blacks. . . . Having been in contact with the life of the towns, they have some measure of political awareness. . . . They can do more for themselves than their completely peasant companions. We must realize, therefore, that this group can be a very important agent for social change in the rural areas.[29]

Hence, for Ndebele, black liberation could only come from a political awareness developed in the urban settings. It was not that urban people were superior to their rural counterpart; on the contrary, as we have shown above, Ndebele himself condemned the urban middle classes for their capitalistic and reactionary ethos. But the point remains that, for Ndebele and most Black Consciousness' advocates, peasants were engulfed in what Marx had called the "idiocy of rural life." An urban intelligentsia, armed with the weapons of critical consciousness, would have to come to the peasants' rescue and activate their revolutionary potential.

However, the urban setting in itself could not cause the rise of this critical consciousness. In a Leninist vein Ndebele suggested that urban workers could not completely understand their own situation if they were not educated by the same revolutionary intelligentsia:

> Like the peasants, the urban workers have a great potential for effecting social change; but they have had no effective leadership. . . . It is the educated middle class who can explain to the workers the working of the system they live in, in order to channel this vast wealth of initiative towards the destruction of the system.[30]

Therefore, what had to be done was, to use Paulo Freire's term the "conscientizacao" of the black masses. The masses were not yet fully aware of the contradictions existing in their own material, moral, and cultural conditions of livelihood and they were therefore incapable of acting against them.[31] The historical role of the Black Consciousness Movement therefore consisted of bringing to the black masses the objective and dialectical knowledge required for their own liberation. The oppressiveness that determined the masses' existence had to become a recognized social reality; that is, it had to be perceived as a transformable condition.

History had to turn into the history of the unceasing destruction of the exploitative manifestations of human creativity. Paulo Freire has identified and clarified this predicament:

> The leaders must believe in the potentialities of the people, whom they cannot treat as mere objects of their own action; they must believe that the people are capable of participating in the pursuit of liberation. But they must always mistrust the ambiguity of oppressed men, mistrust the oppressor "housed" in the later.[32]

The process of becoming conscious should not lead to unrealistic assumptions about the ability of the oppressed to determine their position in the struggle.

What was needed was a strategy whereby the oppressed could participate in the transformation of their environment, not as mere objects or units of labor but as subjects endowed with intelligence and creativity. Only by their active participation in this process of transformation could oppressed people come to realize that many of their own ways of being, behaving, and comprehending contributed to their dehumanization. This realization entails the discovery of "epochal themes" which indicate the series of "aspirations, concerns, and values in search of fulfillment" at a particular period of history.

These "epochal themes" must be grasped and comprehended by the oppressed if they are to act against the oppressive elements of existence. In Freire's analysis:

> Men play a crucial role in the fulfillment and in the superseding of the epochs. Whether or not man can perceive the epochal themes

and above all, how they act upon the reality within which these themes are generated will largely determine their humanization or dehumanization, their affirmation as Subjects or their reduction as objects. For only as men grasp the themes can they intervene in reality instead of remaining mere onlookers.[33]

The Black Community Program (BCP), created in 1972, was based on comparable judgment and was aimed precisely at the conscientizacao of the masses, at dynamizing them towards their liberation. In Mafika Gwala's words:

(The BCP) initiates the principles of self-help and self-determination through inculcating, fostering, directing, maintaining and extending self-reliance in the black community, by encouraging the people in the urban and rural areas to deal with their needs in setting up an appropriate agency or organization with a structure capable of meeting these needs.[34]

The goal of such community projects was not limited to the development of black self-reliance; the idea was also to build a sense of mutual confidence between the leaders and the masses. Without this confidence the unity of black resistance would never be attained, and emancipation would be that more difficult. Nkosazana Dlamini, the last vice-president of SASO, put the point concisely:

If we had tried to explain to an apathetic man: the white man is not your problem as such, your problem is capitalism and imperialism—he wouldn't have known what we were talking about. Now that they are with us—the student body and the mass of people—it is easier to explain the fundamental problems of our struggle in South Africa . . . that our struggle is not really a racial struggle, that we are more concerned about the socio-economic structure.[35]

The community programs therefore served to radicalize the otherwise submissive masses; they offered an understanding of the system and ways to combat it.

However, having launched the community programs, the Black Consciousness Movement was apprehensive that they would evolve towards social reform instead of achieving the wholesale transformation of the South African order. While community programs might well contribute to the alleviation of black poverty, they might as a result ensure the continued existence of a racist and capitalist society. By redressing some social grievances, the black community programs might induce, not revolution, but reformism. In the words of Nengwekhulu:

> We are aware of the fact that the greatest danger inherent in all community development projects designed to bring about change in the community and to instill a sense of self-reliance is that these projects may potentially become welfare projects. . . . In other words, the main purpose of welfare projects is to alleviate the suffering rather than to eradicate the source of the evils. Welfare projects have never brought a revolution and they are not likely to ignite one; in fact they destroy and annihilate all elements necessary for a revolution.[36]

It is therefore obvious that the Movement did not perceive community programs as an altruistic insurance against radical change; on the contrary, they were to be a first step towards revolution. As Nengwekhulu explained: "When we talk of community projects, we mean projects that will revolutionize and transform the entire colonial capitalist society in which we live and thereby to destroy forever the economic exploitation and dependency of our people."[37]

It is difficult to ascertain to what degree these community programs were successful in attaining their goals. According to D. A. Kotze: "Few projects have so far been completed, and the message of Black Consciousness has not been spread very widely in rural African areas."[38] While this claim has a certain plausibility insofar as the rural areas are concerned, it appears that the Movement was much more successful among the urban youth. Several youth organizations dedicated to the furtherance and development of Black Consciousness emerged in the early and mid-1970's.[39] Among those, the one which was to play the most significant role was the South African Student Movement (SASM).

Created in 1972 by Soweto high-school students, SASM committed itself to the overall programs and goals of Black Consciousness. SASM, however, did not originate in SASO; it emerged from the aspirations and struggles of high school students residing primarily in the Transvaal townships.[40] As SASM's General Secretary, Tebello Motapanyane put it:

> It is not correct to say that SASM was an off-shoot of SASO . . . SASM was formed independently and was quite autonomous. Firstly it was not actually spearheaded by SASO people; the decision was taken by people from the youth clubs to cater for the needs of high school students—we did not have in mind to copy what SASO was doing. But many ideas that we used to project like Black Consciousness for instance, SASO was also preaching.[41]

Thus, the seeds of SASM were planted in the youth clubs of three high schools in Soweto—Diepkloof, Orlando and Orlando West. These youth clubs merged to form the African Students Movement (ASM) in April 1971. By 1972, ASM demonstrated its capacity to transcend its Soweto parameters and it changed its name to SASM to indicate its incipient national character. Finally, the seeds of ASM rapidly grew into a National Council of SASM in March 1976. At this time SASM had become a truly national organization with branches in Cape Town, the Transvaal, the Eastern Cape, and possibly Durban. "The main aim of SASM [according to Khoapa was] to coordinate activities of high school students. Their other main areas of operation are their informative programmes concerning injustice in society and in schools and their campaign to preach Black Consciousness."[42]

SASM, however, was more than the vehicle of Black Consciousness among high school students. From its original purpose of serving as a forum for open discussion, SASM evolved into a more militant and structured organization of protest. In this context, it is no surprise that in 1973 the government felt compelled to ban its first Secretary General, the twenty-one year old Mathew Diseko. Moreover, by 1975, SASM developed secret cells where the question of the armed struggle was debated extensively. These cells provided both a link to the exile liberation movement and principally the ANC, and a means of initiating the youngsters into the harsh realities of revolutionary underground activity. In the words of Brooks and Brickhill:

> [By the time of the Soweto uprisings] SASM was fully fledged as a national school student movement, although there must have been numerous small towns or locations where it had not yet established a presence. It had a well-organised structure, a vigorous programme of activities, and a leadership with at least some experience of repression and of clandestine methods of work, at the top levels, if not lower down the line.[43]

It is difficult, however, to know how many members SASM actually had even if there are accounts of open meetings in Soweto branches attended by more than 200 youngsters. Whatever the membership may have been, it is nonetheless clear that SASM had a profound impact on the Soweto uprisings through the Soweto Students Representative Council (SSRC). It was this Council, known at the time as the Action Committee, that planned the demonstration of June 16, 1976 which sparked the uprisings themselves.[44]

Although it would be an exaggeration to declare that these uprisings were the sole responsibility of SASM, it would be hard to overestimate its role in organizing them. As Nengwekhulu pointed out:

> [The uprisings] started in Soweto . . . because that [was] where SASM [had] its head office. SASM . . . [was] predominantly centered in Soweto. The kind of leadership which [was] running it there [was] more radical than the leadership throughout the whole country . . . The uprising started in Soweto, not because those pupils were more oppressed there but because SASM was centered there. The BPC head office [was] also in Soweto and could provide the kind of information there that they could not provide us with in the rest of [the] country. They could meet people and address meetings, so it was easier for them to communicate to the people.[45]

One need not agree with Nengwekhulu's exaggeration of the role of SASM in the historical events of Soweto to accept that it constituted one of the most fundamental factors triggering them. A full understanding of Soweto would require a long and complex analysis of the political, economic, and cultural sphere surrounding the black population, and this goes well beyond the scope of our designs. What concerns us here is the spread of Black Consciousness as revolutionary consciousness throughout black South Africa.

The community programs became one of the essential means through which the Black Consciousness Movement reached the masses to influence the course of history. But these programs, important as they were, could never have produced the degree of critical awareness which ignited Soweto without the active presence of a political party. The Black Peoples Convention (BPC) sought to perform this political function and contributed also to the proselyting of Black Consciousness. The BPC regrouped under its leadership the various organs of Black Consciousness in an effort to strengthen the unity of black resistance. According to Brooks and Brickhill, by 1973 the BPC had forty-one branches throughout South Africa and it probably had a membership of 4,000.[46] As a document presented at the trial of the "SASO Nine" recognized:

> Presently BPC is the only political movement of Blacks for Blacks in this country. It acts as a mother body of all Black organisations— the South African Students Organisation, National Youth Organisation, South African Students Movement, . . . Black Allied Workers Union. . . .[47]

The BPC constitued a unitary front for most Black Consciousness organizations. However, it "never managed to establish itself as a national movement, owing to bannings and harrassment, and remained more or less a collection of activist groups."[48] It is important, nonetheless, to comment further on the BPC's economic policies so as to arrive at a clearer understanding of the material basis of the Black Consciousness Movement.

The BPC's economic strategy rested on the concept of black communalism. Although black communalism represented an economic synthesis in statu nascendi, it is possible to identify its ethical and social undertones. Black communalism provided a coherent formulation for the creation of a new economic system even if its formulation was as yet incomplete and could only provide a foundation for further undertakings. This foundation rested on a reexamination of the African heritage from which the concepts of solidarity, corporate personality, and community ownership emerged as instrumental tools for the building of a modern egalitarian society. In short, black communalism sought to incorporate a revived but revolutionized African tradition into the modern framework of a socialist economy.

The clearest statement of this came from the BPC's convention of 1976:

> BPC adopts Black communalism as its economic policy and Black Communalism can be defined as an economic system which is based on the principle of sharing, lays emphasis on community ownership of land and its wealth and riches; and which strikes a healthy balance between what may legitimately be owned by individuals and what ought to be owned by the community as a whole . . . Black communalism . . . is a modified version of the traditional African economic life-style which is being geared to meet the demands of a highly industrialized and modern economy.
>
> The sharing envisaged will not necessarily be monitored by the State for the benefit of the State itself, but may well be either between groups of individuals or specific communities comprising the State.
>
> As in the traditional outlook . . . sharing shall imply not only the sharing of property and wealth, but also sharing of services and labour. . . .[49]

Black communalism entailed, therefore, a profound transformation of the capitalist economy, and a radical redistribution of wealth between races and classes. As Tami Zani observed,

> The practice whereby the wealth of the country is locked in the hands of a very small greedy minority, will receive attention. Unbridled capitalism has its days numbered throughout the world and there will be no exception in the future of Azania.
>
> A proper redistribution of the wealth of the country also implies that those who have been living on an artificially high standard because of exclusive privileges and opportunities, must be prepared to suffer setbacks in the interests of the national good. We believe

that it is much better for many to make definite progress, though
at a slow pace, than for a few to advance by leaps and bounds, at
the expense of all.[50]

With attitudes comparable to Nyerere's Ujamaa, black communalism did not set out to promote economic miracles and
economic booms of the capitalistic type. Such miracles and
booms were seen to contain a dialectical process of massive
poverty and marginality at one pole, and extreme opulence at
the other. Black communalism was in accord with Denis Goulet's assertion:

> Not to impose equitable austerity on a developing nation is to
> condemn its underprivileged masses to a degrading form of austerity
> whose only beneficiaries are privileged classes and foreign interests.
> . . . If the abolition of poverty is one proper goal of the development
> effort, national austerity must be imposed. . . . Genuine austerity
> within poor countries is the refusal to waste, to practice ostentation,
> or to allow potential resources to lie idle out of inertia.[51]

This type of austerity, however, necessitates the drastic curbing
of the powers of large scale private property and it necessitates
economic planning to suppress the dehumanizing vagaries of
the market. It necessitates the community's control over matters
affecting it. This is why the BPC's black communalism expected
the state to "play a leading role in the planning and development
of industry and commerce."[52] As such, the state was to be
"entrusted" with the control of land, and it was to own the
strategic industries and the major financial institutions of the
nation. However, the state was not to become a leviathan at
the service of a "bureaucratic-bourgeoisie." Its task was to
"protect the interests of workers against exploitation and un-
satisfactory working conditions."[53]

Politically, this meant that "all sane persons shall be eligible
to participate in the making of the laws under which they live,
through the people's National Assembly which shall be a body
constituted of elected representatives of all people."[54] This did
not mean that the Black Consciousness Movement cherished
western bourgeois forms of parliamentary democracy. It is pos-

sible to ascertain that although it never clearly enunciated its vision of democracy, the Movement understood democracy as the adaptation of the tribal political system of ancient Africa to the requirements of a modern socialist society. In this respect, the contemporary philosophies of African socialism as manifested in Nyerere's Ujamaa, in Machel's and Cabral's "Poder Popular," and in Kaunda's "Humanism" were of decisive importance.[55]

It was from these African political experiences and not from Western liberalism that the Black Consciousness Movement drew its inspiration. Indeed, Western liberalism was perceived as alien and individualistic, and ultimately corrupting. In Biko's words,

> In rejecting Western values, therefore, we are rejecting those things that are not only foreign to us but that seek to destroy the most cherished of our beliefs—that the cornerstone of society is man himself—not just his welfare, not his material well-being but just man himself with all his ramifications. . . . We believe that in the long run the special contribution to the world by Africa will be in this field of human relationship.[56]

These considerations, as expressed in Biko's words, introduce us to the ethics of Black Consciousness which were rooted in the Judeo-Christian tradition. While this tradition had been introduced with the Western colonial impact, the Christianity of the Black Consciousness Movement embodied the negation of the dominant religious bourgeois ethos. As such it acquired a black "specificity" which was expressed in the elaboration of a new Black Theology.

Chapter V

Black Theology

Black Theology is in revolt against the spiritual enslavement of black people, and thus against the loss of their sense of human dignity and worth. It is a theology by which to affirm black humanity. It is a theology of the oppressed, by the oppressed, for the liberation of the oppressed.[1]

So Basil Moore, a Methodist clergyman and a past general secretary of the University Christian Movement (UCM), defined Black Theology. Black Theology served as a revolutionary ethic for the emancipation of the black masses and was considered by blacks as synonymous with genuine Christianity. In this sense, Christianity was the dialectical ethic of a prophetic movement determined to abolish the social, cultural, and moral bases of exploitation. In South Africa, Christianity flourished only when it contributed to the realization of black liberation.

Black Theology expressed the radical need to resuscitate Christianity from the stultifying grip of colonial and racist domination in order to restore its original prophetic essence. Christianity, according to the dominant theme of Black Theology, was imbued with the legacy of Jesus' identification with the oppressed, and

Jesus' condemnation of the powers that be. In Sabelo Ntwasa's words,

> Black Theology describes Christ as a fighting God, not a passive God who allows a lie to exist unchallenged. Black Theology grapples with existential problems and does not claim to be a theology of absolutes. It seeks to return God to the black man and to the truth and reality of his situation.[2]

Since Christianity had been usurped by a racist and capitalist world and had accepted dehumanizing forms of class relations, it was up to blacks, up to the oppressed, to renew it and to make of it what it once was—the prophetic world-view of the wretched of the earth. Nietzsche's contention that Christianity was essentially a religion of slaves and the "sacrifice of all freedom, all pride, all self-assurance of the mind"[3] represented an accurate conception not of the historical Jesus and early Christianity, but of what Christianity became as it unfolded under the hegemony of bourgeois-colonial relations and bourgeois consciousness.

In the judgment of Black Theology, the Christianity which accompanied colonization and legitimized colonization itself, was the powerful voice of conservatism and human submission. This perverted Christianity became a cruel instrument by which the white race exploited the black race; it facilitated subjection and sought to destroy the humanness of the black people. As Basil Moore explained:

> In South Africa the Christian Church has probably been one of the most powerful instruments in making possible the political oppression of the black people. . . . [The] Church made it plain that everything African was heathen and superstitious barbarism. Conversion to Christianity meant rejecting traditional forms of dress, authority, social organization, culture, marriage, medicine, etc. The black people were made to believe not that salvation is in Christ alone, but that salvation is in accepting the new white ways of living. The effect of this was to internalize in the black people a sense of the inferiority which inhered in them as Africans.[4]

Therefore, the history of the colonial church was a history of active support of the social and economic initiatives of white conquest. It preached not liberation and salvation of the oppressed, but obedience and submission to immoral forms of domination. It distorted the teachings of Christ, as it sided Him with the oppressor and not with the poor and the oppressed. For Black Theology, the Christianity that became attached to the white power system falsified the real Christianity of the historical Jesus. Yet, if the colonial church contributed greatly to the enslavement of the black population, it could not strip, despite desperate efforts, the revolutionary and prophetic content from both the Old and New Testaments.

The doctrine of equality before God, the element of transcendence inherent in obedience to powers beyond the human realm, could only dissolve the ideological bases which supported the grim inequality of man before man, that is, the black man's unqualified submission to earthly masters. By portraying the historical Jesus as a revolutionary bent on eradicating exploitation, Black Theology sought to redirect Christianity towards the liberation of the oppressed. In the words of James Cone, the black American theologian whose writings did much to inspire the rise of Black Theology in South Africa,

> Jesus is not safely confined in the first century. He is our contemporary, proclaiming release to the captives and rebelling against all who silently accept the structures of injustice. If he is not in the ghetto, if he is not where men are living at the brink of existence, but is, rather, in the easy life of the suburbs, then the gospel is a lie.[5]

It is in this sense that Black Theology's "cri du coeur" that "Christ is Black" must be understood. This did not necessarily imply that god was the exclusive possession of black people.

While Cone came close to espousing such exclusivity, Black Theology in South Africa rejected it. It is true that in the South African context, the only meaningful manifestation of Christianity found expression in Black Theology; but this is a far cry from claiming God "solely for the black experience." As Allan Boesak, the black South African theologian, observed:

> We submit that to make black as such the symbol of oppression and liberation in the world is to absolutise the own situation. . . .

> Cone's mistake is that he has taken Black Theology out of the
> framework of the theology of liberation, thereby making the own
> situation (being black in America) and the own movement (liber-
> ation from white racism) the ultimate criterion for all theology. By
> doing this, Cone makes of a contextual theology a regional theology
> which is not the same thing at all. . . . Indeed, Black Theology is
> a theology of liberation in the situation of blackness. For blacks,
> it is the only legitimate way of theologizing—*but only within the
> framework of the theology of liberation.*[6]

Thus, "Christ is Black" was not a symptom of a racist backlash
gone wild, but rather the immanent necessity of placing the
universal experience of oppression in the context of the South
African reality. Jesus, by identifying with the poor, and by
accepting his down-graded, Jewish status had shown the way;
He had sided with the oppressed. If He were alive today in
South Africa, He would therefore be black.[7]

To say that "Christ is Black," however, is not merely to claim
that God addresses himself primarily to the oppressed. It is
much more than that; it is to claim that the struggle for black
emancipation stems directly from God's authority. The politically radical and the morally subversive legacy that the historical
Jesus bequeathed, strengthened and indeed legitimized the revolutionary inclination of Black Theology and hence of the Black
Consciousness Movement. By constantly struggling to deliver
man from the bondages of this world, Jesus embodied the
promise of freedom and indeed the promise of the kingdom of
God on earth:

> To see the revelation of God is to see the action of God in the
> historical affairs of men. God is not uninvolved in human history.
> . . . The opposite is true: he is participating in human history,
> moving in the direction of man's salvation which is the goal of
> divine activity.[8]

But if human liberation stems from divine activity, are people
not abdicating their own powers; are they not denying their
own freedom? If human beings are to be independent and free
beings, should they not detach themselves from their dependency

on a transcendental and omnipotent God? Should they not negate His very existence? As Robert Birt has put it:

> If man is a creature of God, his creator, it follows then that man is not a being for himself, but being for his divine master. If God is the source of my being, then that could quite logically mean that I am a slave of God. . . . If God replaces white people as the source of my being, then I have merely exchanged masters.[9]

This view of Christianity was rejected by Black Theology as a narrow and one-sided indictment of a larger problem. The existence of God as creator was not per se an abdication of freedom; rather human beings were co-creators with God in history. Since the Word of God reaches humanity through human history, it is no wonder that to each historical period corresponds a new revelation. It is precisely in the ushering in of new historical periods, created by human activity, that the kingdom's growth is assured. Gustavo Gutierrez, a major figure in the development of the theology of liberation, argued as follows:

> The growth of the Kingdom is a process which occurs historically in liberation, insofar as liberation means a greater fulfillment of man . . . Moreover, we can say that the historical, political liberating event is the growth of the Kingdom and is a salvific event; but it is not the coming of the Kingdom, not all of salvation.[10]

Thus, Black Theology as a theology of liberation did not deny the freedom of men and women, but the absoluteness of their freedom. Black Theology maintained the limitations of human beings as the products of particular historical cultures and so took a stance against the pitfalls of triumphalism. This is a far cry from theological conceptions of man as an historically passive creature subservient to God's inscrutable will, a view which was attacked by Sabelo Ntwasa and Basil Moore in "The Concept of God in Black Theology":

> Black Theology is as irrelevant as any other theology if it is not about human liberation, and thus about black liberation. It must

> therefore explore new symbols of God which affirm human au-
> thenticity, freedom and wholeness. The old images of God as
> 'Person,' 'over' or 'beyond' us, will no longer do.[11]

As free agents, the oppressed look longingly toward delivery
from earthly bondage; they seek redemption not in some remote
heaven but in the kingdom of God which is struggling to exist
in history, in this world. The historical role of Black Theology
therefore became the articulation of a message of revolutionary
hope. This hope gestated in the material, cultural, and moral
manifestations of the black existential condition. It is in this
emphasis on praxis that Black Theology differentiated itself from
a purely "African theology."

With its tendency to romanticize the African past, African
theology embodied an ethnic approach which sought a nostalgic
Africanization instead of liberation. In Buthelezi's words,

> Too much emphasis is placed upon the African world-view as if
> it were an isolated and independent entity apart from the present
> anthropological reality of the African man. The quest for an in-
> digenous theology seems to be understood as originating from the
> problem of a conflict between two-world-views: the European and
> the African. The human factor seems to recede to the background,
> if recognized at all. . . . For these reasons the 'ethnographic' ap-
> proach to indigenous theology falls short. For theology to be in-
> digenous, it is not enough that it should deal merely with 'African
> things' like the African world-view; it must also reflect the life
> dynamics of the present-day African.[12]

Appropriately, Black Theology drew its intellectual and moral
ethic not only from the gospel and the African religious tradition,
but also from the conditions surrounding blackness and oppression. Thus, the religious phenomenon emanated not as the
shaper, but as the transcendental product of the worldly world.
As Buthelezi put it: "The Word of God reaches man in his
real situation, which may not always be an ideal one."[13]

Hence, the struggle for freedom was not to be envisaged as
the struggle for reestablishing the hegemony of the African
tradition. There was an inherent danger in the nostalgic longing
for reviving a yesterday that had lost much of its relevance.

This hindered the necessary analysis of the contemporary black problem, and aroused false hopes and illusions in the black mind. As David Bosch has argued in a few convincing short strokes about William Eteki-Mboumoua's theology:

> If we now, in the modern period, attempt a revival of archaic patterns of life, we run the risk of merely creating disembodied caricatures of once significant and functional institutions. We should then be producing "Zombis". . . .[14]

This rejection of a complete return to traditional forms of African culture and politics was by no means a rejection of the concept of African specificity. Indeed, what ran through Black Theology was a profound criticism of Western bourgeois in-dividualism and a dramatic call to rescue both black and white people from its dehumanizing grips. The African specificity based on corporate personality and communalism was seen as the ethical solution to the alienation of modern men and women. In other words, Africans had as their historical mission the task of humanizing the disfigured, individualistic white world.[15]

However, in South Africa the human situation was determined by race, and the gospel had therefore to relate first to the exploited black before it could extend an effective universalist message of reconciliation to white people. Indeed, the Gospel had to become the property of the oppressed in their struggle against earthly bondage. "As such [Motlhabi argued] God is neither our servant, to be treated as we choose, nor our master, to treat us as he chooses, but our comrade and friend in the struggle for freedom."[16]

This vision of Black Theology was the negation of what Biko called the "cold and cruel religion"[17] of white Christians; it was a Christian search for human community that finds expression in man-made liberating events and the fusion of the profane and the sacred. It was a search that echoed Karl Barth's an-thropocentric Christian understanding that "Man is the measure of all things, since God became man."[18] In short, Black Theology was Christian worldliness; the struggle for God's kingdom in history.

This led to radical criticisms of the Church which found itself within society and yet constantly strove to remain other-worldly, that is, outside the historical struggles of human praxis. Not surprisingly, Black Theology condemned the artificial division between the secular and the religious, and the profane and the sacred. The striving for perfection in *this* world was a necessity to which the Church had to contribute decisively. To do otherwise would "[obstruct] the effectiveness of the Church's mission and [retard] or utterly [obscure] the understanding of the Scriptures."[19]

Based on this type of analysis, Black Theology was therefore an attempt to rescue the Church and Christianity from their overt or silent collusion with exploiting structures of power. If it failed in this mission, then Christianity and the Church would, at best be irrelevant for the black struggle; at worst they would represent a hostile bastion of reaction that would have to be crushed. The Church could no longer afford to live in comfortable detachment from political life and the search for justice; it had to risk itself in seeking the transformation of this world. Furthermore, Christianity must not, as John de Gruchy sees it, discover in Marxism "the growing power of a hostile ideology,"[20] and withdraw from a potentially constructive dialogue.

On the contrary, Christianity must start reflecting on the anthropomorphic dimensions of the Marxist legacy, its major sociological insights, and the hope inherent in its revolutionary spirit. To do otherwise was to condemn the Church to irrelevancy. In the words of Boesak, this meant,

> . . . that the Church ought to discover that the state of poverty and oppression is ugly, impermissible and unnecessary; that conditions of poverty and underdevelopment are not metaphysical but structural and historically explicable. In other words, poverty is one side of a coin of which the other side is affluence and exploitation. The Church must needs discover that oppressed people are not merely loose individuals but a class. . . . While absolutely not minimizing racism as a demonic, pseudo-religious ideology, (who coming from South Africa, can?) we must nonetheless ask: Is racism indeed the only issue? It seems to us that there is a far deeper malady in the American and South African societies that manifests itself in the form of racism . . . the relation between racism and capitalism. . . .[21]

It is no wonder, therefore, that for Black Theology there could be no Christian reconcilation between blacks and whites within the existing capitalist structures. The dissolution of bourgeois class relations constituted an essential precondition for reconciliation between the races. The pseudo-reconciliation which was occurring in capitalist South Africa was perverted by its elitist and hypocritical character. For Moore the diagnosis was clear:

> . . . the 'reconciliation' that took place was phony. What happened in effect was that 'class' loyalty took over from race loyalty. Black and white distinctions paled before the common bond of wealth and education. . . . Having this class character the effect of multi-racialism was to draw the upper crust of black society off from the masses and then to graft it on to the white middle-to-upper class. But the illiterate, poor and starving black masses were left as leaderless as ever. . . . 'Reconciliation' between the races has been gained, if at all, at the expense of 'reconciliation' between the potential black leaders and the forgotten black masses. This, above all else has been the black tragedy of our middle class multiracialism.[22]

Thus, although Black Theology was certainly not based on Marxist categories and analysis, it is clear that the material and cultural conditions of black existence convinced its spokesmen of the need for class analysis and of the inherent structural injustices of capitalism. This secular content of Black Theology may have in fact checked a massive withdrawal from South African Christianity. The truth of Mafeje's claim that young militants "are destined to produce the necessary revolutionary paradigms, [and that the] . . . issue will be resolved neither in the church nor on Zion but in the wider society which the radicals have chosen as their terrain,"[23] does not contradict this. Rather, the revolutionary paradigms being applied in the "wider society" are essentially in harmony with the vision of Black Theology. Black Theology was a radical vision of human striving for realization on earth, even if it had not yet fully worked out the thoroughly revolutionary interdependencies of Christianity and socialism. Eugene Genovese's remarks on the black religion of the American slaves complement this understanding of Black Theology's function in contemporary South Africa:

> Black religion, understood as a critical world-view in the process of becoming—as something unfinished, often inconsistent, and in some respects even incoherent—emerged as the slaves' most formidable weapon for resisting slavery's moral and psychological aggression. Without it or its moral equivalent, 'day-to-day resistance to slavery' might have been condemned to the level of a pathetic nihilism, incapable of bridging the gap between individual action against an oppressor and the needs of the collective for self-discipline, community elan, and a sense of worth as a people rather than merely as a collection of individuals. With it, the slaves were able to struggle, by no means always successfully, for collective forms of resistance in place of individual outburst.[24]

A final and essential ethical issue remains to be discussed. If Black Theology offered a promise of deliverance in this world, how and by what means would this promise materialize in history? Indeed, if the ultimate aim of Black Theology was the liberation of the oppressed and if the oppressors were bent on preserving the system of oppression to which they owed their privileged status, would not liberation entail violent confrontation? Did Black Theology's insistence on the cultural and economic liberation of the oppressed carry within it the inevitable moral legitimation of violence?

Disdaining revolutionary violence and advocating a spiritual revolution, Black Theology believed that the radical transformation of society could stem from the diffusion of a prophetic Christian consciousness. By interpreting the world from a prophetic perspective and by sharing this interpretation with both black and white people, Black Theology hoped that violence could be avoided or at least minimized in the revolutionary process. Black Theology felt a strong commitment to free the whites from their spiritual madness and from their dehumanizing consciousness. Manas Buthelezi advocated the creation of a black Christian mission to the whites "to work for the salvation of the white man who sorely needs it."[25] He also stated: "It is now time for the black man to evangelize and humanize the white man. The realization of this will not depend on the white man's approval, but solely on the black man's love for the white man."[26] Thus, the kingdom of God on earth could be nurtured through the black-induced transformation of white attitudes.

Yet, it is clear that Black Theology was sophisticated enough to understand the limitations of a prophetic and critical consciousness in the revolutionary process if it was not linked to praxis. In this respect, Black Theology was haunted by the equivalent of Max Weber's observation: "The decisive means for politics is violence."[27] The issue was therefore whether praxis should embrace violence and whether violence might fracture existing structures of injustice and create a more humane society. While Black Theology stopped short of advocating violence, it experienced the tensions of preaching a critical consciousness that fell on the deaf ears of the whites, while simultaneously activating the revolutionary potential of the blacks and the possibility of violent insurrection.

In this context, several spokesmen for Black Theology clung rather desperately to the hope of peaceful revolution and vigorously condemned the advocates of violence. Criticizing the American theologian Joseph Washington, Boesak wrote:

> . . . in Washington's thinking power comes out of the barrel of a gun and this is . . . a falsification of authentic power. Nowhere does Washington seem to take into account that violence, once unleashed, acquires an autonomy of its own of which the inseparable twin is escalation. Whereas Washington does not seem to care about hatred ever deepening, nor about the escalation of inhumanity through more and more violence, we do. All in all, Washington's thinking is so strongly reminiscent of the ideology of the ruling class that we cannot but reject it outrightly.[28]

Be that as it may, Black Theology could not put up with blacks being the perpetual victims of exploitation. However unwillingly, it had to envisage violence as a regrettable and inevitable if not morally justifiable agent of revolution, given the intransigence of South Africa's white power structure. Indeed, Black Theology painfully came to the conclusion that in South Africa the victims of oppression had only two options: either to suffer the institutionalized violence of white supremacy, or resist injustice with minimal but effective violence. While neither option seemed to be morally justifiable, there was a qualitative distinction between the violence of the oppressor and the violence of the oppressed.

While the former was seen to be inherently dehumanizing and beyond redemption, the latter might hopefully carry with it the liberation which would purge society of the existing structures of injustice, so providing a new opportunity for future generations. However, even this hope did not fully relieve the tension, and black theologians did not explicitly accept Freire's claim that the violence of the oppressed would "initiate love [and would] restore to the oppressors the humanity they had lost in the exercise of oppression."[29] In Boesak's words,

> Whereas we do not deny that a situation may arise where retaliatory violence is forced upon the oppressed and no other avenue is left open to them, we do so with a clear hesitancy, knowing full well that it will probably prove a poor 'solution' and that violence can never be 'justified.'[30]

Thus, because of the Christian, generous, and perhaps naive impulses of Black Theology, it could not harden itself to preach violence. Yet these attributes were precisely what imbued it with the ethical and spiritual dimension so necessary for the ultimate fulfillment of a truly liberating revolution. Black Theology displayed shrewd human judgment in drawing attention to the stark and often overlooked reality that violence and the coming of black liberation "will not eliminate all grief and sadness, unhappy love affairs or mourning, and will not solve or make soluble all problems."[31]

Far from precluding the emergence of an ideology of hope and breaking the black revolutionary élan, Black Theology's Christian understanding of human limitations in history laid the basis not for passivity and contemplation, but for a revolutionary praxis embedded in a deep sense of humility. This was not the humility of shame and submission, but the marvelous sense of being human, black, and proud of it. Black Theology therefore sparked the ethical renaissance of black men and black women; it fired them with the almost forgotten feeling of their own worth and their own humanity. It enabled them to save themselves from the white-bourgeois cultic ethos and to lay the foundations for a new black identity and a new black culture.

This culture was to express a dialectical duality in being both the outgrowth of black existential conditions and a universal statement of potential liberation for all oppressed people. Black Theology in this perspective was to help build the collective strength of the oppressed and provide them with a moral yardstick with which to judge the extent of white injustice. Simultaneously its unbounded commitment to love provided a glimpse of the ultimate earthly transcendence: the universal communion and universal sisterhood/brotherhood of all human beings. Black Theology compelled the oppressed to envisage reconciliation with their white enemies, even if it simultaneously and unconsciously propelled both to the violent confrontation of a protracted struggle. So, whatever inconsistencies and contradictions may have plagued Black Theology, they did not destroy its central message of worldly liberation and Christian reconciliation.

The emergence of Black Theology had therefore shown that the center of gravity of black thinking had shifted away from the fatalism of a superimposed "colonial Christianity," as well as from the millenarianism of Zionism and Ethiopianism. Expressing the religious sensibility of the new ideological radicalism, Black Theology became the indispensable moral ingredient of the Black Consciousness Movement. The aspirations of the black intelligentsia for economic transformations and cultural hegemony as against the exploitative and paternalistic structures of apartheid society induced the development of a prophetic consciousness; Black Theology was the ethical consequence. Inseparably bound together, Black Theology and Black Consciousness expressed the radical thrust of a struggle for the abolition of material and moral deprivations, and the establishment of more humane relationships. It remains to be seen whether this interdependency between Black Theology and Black Consciousness will withstand the severe pressures of the protracted struggle against white supremacy.

Chapter VI

Conclusions and Assessments

On October 19, 1977, the Internal Security Act banned SASO, BPC, and all the Black Consciousness Movement organizations.[1] The previous month Biko was murdered by the security police; he was the forty-fourth black to die in this way. This major crackdown on the Black Consciousness Movement illustrated the futility of peaceful protest in the face of a repressive and intransigent white power structure. It demonstrated that the black struggle was bound to arouse the fiercest enmity from the white, privileged minority. From the advent of the Movement in 1969 and after, black resistance became more and more threatening, especially as it sparked the revolutionary awakening of the black intellect and challenged existing capitalist relations.

By the mid-1970's, the white state resorted once again to the pervasive use of overt force to protect the status-quo. This is not to deny that the threat of institutional violence has always been in the background as a means of dissuasion, but rather to point that the renewed vigor of African resistance could no longer be squashed by the cultural hegemony of white supremacy. Hegemony was clearly incapable of sustaining the structures of white dominance; now the overt use of force would decisively supplant it. The violent suppression of African resistance became a fundamental element of what emerged as the Total Strategy of the white state. This strategy, proclaimed by General Magnus Malan in the 1977 Defense White Paper, stemmed from what the managers of apartheid described as the "total onslaught" waged against white South Africa. In these circumstances, the survival of white dominance required the adoption of an all-encompassing strategy coordinating state policies at the political, economic, diplomatic, and cultural levels. The Total Strategy was thus defined as:

> . . . the comprehensive plan to utilize all the means available to an integrated pattern in order to achieve the national aims within the framework of the specific policies. A total strategy is, therefore, not confined to a particular sphere, but is applicable at all levels and to all functions of the state structure.[2]

Hence military and paramilitary actions were to be combined with the exercise of statecraft in its most general sense. Force was to be used to create a new terrain in which a restructuration of politics, culture, and economics could be effected in order to co-opt and divide the black opposition. The defenders of apartheid were in the process of implementing a "passive revolution" bent on reforming from above, the terms of white supremacy. On the one hand Africans were to be treated unequally in an effort to divide them into conflicting social strata, and on the other Asians and "Coloureds" were to be partially integrated into the white political system in an effort to draw them away from potential alliances with the African majority. Finally, these political maneuvers were to be protected and indeed implemented by the threat and/or the decisive use of force.

To a large extent this restructuring of white dominance was the direct consequence of the travail of the Black Consciousness Movement; a travail which did not end, however, with the state imposed bannings. Indeed, Black Consciousness is still a movement possessed of great vitality;[3] it is still in the process of defining itself. The Movement, however, acquired a revolutionary ethic in the course of the 1970's. Thus, the widely accepted interpretation of Black Consciousness as a middle-class intellectual movement[4] not seriously bent on "contemplating . . . revolutionary changes,"[5] is quite incorrect given a careful analysis of its ideology. The 1976 massive uprising in Soweto appears to confirm this. Moreover, when René Lefort claims that Black Consciousness was an essentially populist movement trying to escape from a materialistic understanding of the South Africa reality, he commits a serious error.[6] For, as I have shown, the Movement was not only well aware of the class-ridden and capitalistic nature of South African society, it was also determined to abolish both.

Yet, it is true that the Black Consciousness Movement had neither strong organizational ties with the working class, nor did it develop direct linkages with one of the leading forces of the Soweto rebellion—the South African Students Movement (SASM) from which originated the Soweto Students' Representative Council (SSRC). Such organizational weaknesses resulted in a disjunction between the struggles of the youth and the aspirations of the proletarian masses. The wave of industrial strikes of 1973 and 1974 which enhanced the workers' self-confidence and which continued well into 1976 developed largely autonomously and apart from the BCM and the youth's insurrection.

The Black Workers' Union (BAWU) formed in August 1972 as the working class organization of the Black Consciousness Movement, had a limited impact on African proletarians.[7] It never mobilized them in great numbers and it was ill-equipped to become the vanguard of a revolution. As Baruch Hirson remarked: "The workers did not seem to believe that there was any benefit to be derived from joining BAWU."[8]

Similar problems contributed to the difficulties in uniting workers and youth in a common strategy of emancipation. In fact, these difficulties, coupled with the absence of a proletarian party, prevented the narrow "economism" of the workers' strikes of the mid-1970's to grow into an all encompassing political revolution. Thus, when the SSRC called for the workers to go on strike, it was often confronted by the laborers' unwillingness to cooperate. This resistance, encouraged by white authorities and the police, became violent when the migrant workers of the Mzimhlope hostel[9] rampaged the streets of Soweto in their search to kill any rebellious youngsters. While this incident was not generalized, it symbolized the tensions and divisions separating workers from youth.

The youth's calls for political strikes implied major sacrifices for workers in terms of wages and job-security and they never embodied a well-planned revolutionary program. Not surprisingly, they failed to gain the total and generalized support of the working class. The lack of unity and coordination between the youth and the workers repressed the radical potential of the Soweto rebellion which turned into a failed revolution. As Hirson put it:

> [The workers'] lack of formal organisation was to be a weakness, and the need to alter course and transform their economic struggle into a political struggle could not be met. In fact, political strikes were later called by the youth of Soweto, in August and September 1976, but for reasons not directly connected with the demands of workers. The disjunction of purpose by youth and workers when those political stoppages were proposed meant that the struggle could not advance to a higher level. It is just feasible that a well organised working class would have joined the calls to stay at home in 1976, but there was little organisation and the workers of Natal remained outside the orbit of the Revolt.[10]

The clear organizational deficiencies of both the working class and the rebellious youth does not, however, reflect negatively on the pervasive and decisive ideological impact of the Black Consciousness Movement on the making of the Soweto revolt. While the revolt was probably not an "organised mass struggle" as Brooks and Brickhill would have it,[11] it symbolized none-theless the emergence of Black Consciousness as a revolutionary consciousness. The perceptions and aspirations of the Soweto students articulated an unambiguous revolutionary determination: they were embedded in the realization that the abolition of apartheid required the formation of proletarian organizations and proletarian power.[12] For instance, in a leaflet addressed to the working class, the students declared:

> 1. We call on the workers to strike in protest against a slave system and in *solidarity* with all oppressed and exploited groups . . .
> 2. The barbarous state repression of peaceful demonstration tragically underlines that *fundamental changes by the rulers* is a pipe dream.
> 3. Workers are compelled in defence and in pursuit of a better life to call into being worker organisations in the locations and in the factories.
> 4. The situation demands that the oppressed and exploited rally around the slogans of WORKER POWER AND PEOPLES POWER.[13]

Thus, if the Black Consciousness Movement and SASM were both plagued by organizational problems and with a certain incapacity to mobilize and guide the oppressed classes, their message and ideology imparted to their politics a definite revolutionary flavor. The making of a revolution requires not only organization but also a process of ideological diffusion whereby the hegemony of the dominant classes is disarticulated and ultimately displaced by a new philosophy of emancipation. The Black Consciousness Movement effected precisely such disarticulation and displacement and it implanted into black South Africa a new ideological terrain—a terrain in which the organizations and strategies of black resistance will plant their roots, and in which the development and radicalization of black revolutionaries will take place.

It is wrong to conclude that the Black Consciousness Movement was of little significance in the making of Soweto and the rise of a new African militancy against white supremacy. In fact, such a conclusion reflects a unilateral stress on the power of organization and it negates the decisive influence of ideologies in the mobilization of human beings struggling to overthrow exploitative structures.[14] Thus, to view Black Consciousness as a movement of little historical significance and of miminal revolutionary essence is misleading. Despite its organizational weaknesses and its relative immaturity, the Black Consciousness Movement is animated by a revolutionary will and vision.

To view Black Consciousness otherwise is the result of an excessive concentration on its organizational deficiencies, and on Biko's writings and theses. While Biko's bold and determined leadership warrants such attention, it must be recalled that his intellectual impact was checked by his banning and subsequent murder. It has to be recognized that, as far as his writings reveal, Biko was absorbed by the cultural and psychological aspects of black liberation; he failed to analyze in any systematic way the issues of class and economics. What needs to be brought into focus is that however important they may have been, Biko's ideas expressed only the formative and underdeveloped conceptions of the Movement. They represented a truncated and immature current of a larger and more radical ideological flow. Thus, it is erroneous to assume that Biko's world-view is the world-view of the Black Consciousness Movement.

Black Consciousness should be understood as the ethico-political weapon of an oppressed class struggling to reaffirm its humanity through its active participation in the demise of a racist, capitalist society. Raymond Franklin's observations on American black power apply with added force to South African Black Consciousness:

> The ideology of Black Power represents the most advanced articulation of the middle-class Negro's awareness that any salvation worthy of its name must begin with developing a revolutionary consciousness and organization among the Negro working class.[15]

It is also important to draw attention to the often overlooked fact that the Movement could not openly display the extent of its revolutionary commitment, since this would have been suicidal in authoritarian South Africa. Yet, in spite of its caution and circumspection, the Black Consciousness Movement could not escape the logic of its own radicalism and the popular pressures it generated. The bannings testify to the vigor of the Movement as well as its radical opposition to apartheid.

From this perspective, the white liberal criticisms of Black Consciousness become comprehensible. The late, widely-respected liberal Leo Marquard's characterization of Black Consciousness as a "self seeking doctrine" which "thrives by the oppression of other groups,"[16] is fallacious and implicit proof of liberalism's failure to accept the prospect of a revolution of the oppressed. Several leading white liberals also claimed that Black Consciousness was a throwback from the possible advances of multiracialism and that it was a "reverse racism" and an "unmitigated evil."[17] Biko went to the heart of the matter in rejecting the liberals' view of integration which lay behind these criticisms:

> It is an integration in which black will compete with black, using each other as rungs on a step ladder leading them to white values. It is an integration in which the black man will have to prove himself in terms of these values before meriting acceptance and ultimate assimilation, and in which the poor will grow poorer and the rich richer in a country where the poor have always been black.[18]

Black Consciousness rejected the gradualist and ultimately exploitative norms of white liberalism. Likewise it would not tolerate the dictate of white paternalists nor the hegemony of white bourgeois culture which it attacked with passion. The circumspect and patient politics of earlier generations in African politics, dating back at least to the founding of the ANC in 1912, had given way once again to a new forcefulness. As African leaders had become disillusioned with white liberals in the late 1930's and 1940's,[19] and as the Congress Youth League had rejected white hegemony in 1943, so now the Black Consciousness Movement turned away from compromise and the liberal niceties of politics within the established order. As SASO editorialized in late 1975, "All that is needed now is an executioner. And gravediggers."[20] Although these words expressed a naive optimism, they indicated the presence of a revolutionary landmark in the struggle against apartheid and white capitalism. In Biko's words: "To stop us now they will have to kill us all first."[21]

However, under the increasing powers of white repression, the African revolution faced staggering obstacles. The peaceful and legal efforts of past generations had achieved no fundamental change, and there was no guarantee that the adoption of revolutionary means would bring about the desired set of social arrangements. The prospects for immediate revolutionary transformations in South Africa remained somber, but the history of African resistance to colonial exploitation has taught us that even in the most difficult conditions, despair and fatalism had always given way to hope and struggle. So, while the timing and final outcome of resistance to injustice may be in doubt, the rise of the Black Consciousness Movement indicated that white supremacy was showing signs of vulnerability and exhaustion.

Such vulnerability and exhaustion became apparent with the social explosion of 1976 in Soweto. This represented a new phase in the black revolutionary struggle and became a historical landmark, a general rehearsal of things to come.[22] The Soweto uprising was the inevitable outcome of the ideological erosion of the white supremacist order. In this sense Soweto embodied the moral/intellectual period of the revolutionary process, or what Gramsci called the "war of position."[23] In this war of position, the fundamental objective is not the conquest of state power as such, but the frontal assault on the cultural and ideological hegemony of the ruling classes. It is this negation of the dominant system of beliefs that generates a revolutionary situation and a new historical horizon. Black Consciousness, as it destroyed the colonial ethos which strangled the masses' freedom and will, diffused a counter-hegemony which transformed hitherto apathetic men and women into potentially revolutionary subjects.

While the war of position symbolized a historical struggle for ideological supremacy and leadership, it inevitably suffered setbacks arising from the absence of a unified force of professional revolutionaries. As the struggle moved from the cultural sphere to the clashes of actual confrontation, it demonstrated the serious limitations imposed by the inherited structures and agents of the war of position. Since these structures and agents emanated from the confrontation for ideological hegemony, they lacked the military and political organization which was indispensable for waging the "war of movement"[24] and seizing state power.

Hence, while Black Consciousness represented the essential element of the war of position which culminated in the uprisings of Soweto, it was ill-equipped for the transition to revolutionary violence. With Soweto, the Black Consciousness Movement accomplished its historical task: it united to an unprecedented extent the exploited ethnies into a popular bloc, and it diffused a new ideology of liberation which decisively eroded the hegemony of white supremacist mythology. What it could not do was to carry the black majority to power. The road to black communalism was no longer blocked by the mental and psychological enslavement of the masses; it was blocked by the open repressiveness of the white state.

The conquest of power was clearly not just a matter of consciousness and war of position; it required careful preparation for guerrilla warfare itself. And this, more than anything else, demonstrated the limitations of the Black Consciousness Movement. The ideological attacks on white racism were not enough, they inevitably failed to overthrow it. Therefore, to seek to abolish apartheid through ideological criticism was a necessary but wholly insufficient step. Mere exposure of the racist practices of the South African government did not and could not remove them. As Marx long ago declared, "The philosophers have only interpreted the world, in various ways; the point, however, is to change it." And this necessarily requires the full exercise of revolutionary praxis—an exercise which went beyond the organizational and political capacities of the Black Consciousness Movement.

The search for more effective means of struggle led 4,000 students to flee South Africa in 1976 for the training camps of the exiled liberation movement and in particular those of the African National Congress (ANC).[25] However, some of the youngsters of Soweto rejected integration into the established expatriate groups; they formed the Black Consciousness Movement of Azania which moved towards an increasingly socialist direction. Meeting in April 1980 in London, the Black Consciousness Movement of Azania enunciated what amounts to the most radical Declaration of Principles of all the South African liberation organizations. This Declaration of Principles embodied a clear socialist commitment and it stated, among other things, the following points:

> (1) The National Democratic Revolution is based upon the minimum demands of the oppressed masses of Azania, namely, the reconquest of all our land and its resources and the attainment of full democratic rights.
> (2) The Black Consciousness Movement recognizes that the national oppression of our people is a direct result of capitalism and imperialism and thus our struggle is both anti-capitalist and anti-imperialist.
> (3) The Black Consciousness Movement consequently adopts the theory and practice of scientific socialism to guide it in the struggle.
> (4) However, because of the structural and institutionalized nature of the racism in the South African social system, the class struggle continues and will continue to manifest itself in colour terms, and for this reason, we continue to believe in the mobilizing role of Black Consciousness in the struggle in which the black people rally against their common oppression.
> (5) In response to the popular struggles of the masses . . . the South African regime [is making] overtures to the black middle class. This underscores the class essence of the struggle against national oppression.
> (6) The Black Consciousness Movement of Azania recognizes that the black workers are the most oppressed and exploited section of our society, and therefore, constitute the major force in our struggle. Thus the strategy for the revolution should be based on the historical, political and organizational experience of the black working class.[26]

This commitment to socialism was enhanced by the radicalization of the Azanian People's Organisation (AZAPO) which had close links to the Black Consciousness Movement of Azania. Indeed according to its vice-president, Saths Cooper, AZAPO constituted the "vanguard of the black working class" and as such it was "fighting against the stark reality of white racism, fuelled by capitalism and imperialism."[27] While AZAPO's strategy of liberation was embedded in the principles of the class struggle, it was a struggle which manifested itself in racial terms, given the reality of apartheid. Not surprisingly AZAPO's identification of South Africa as a 'racial capitalism' implied the continuation of the earlier Black Consciousness policy of 'going it alone.' Indeed, AZAPO rejected the integration of whites into the movement of liberation. This rejection has accentuated the tensions and conflicts dividing the internal black opposition in South Africa. The old issue of the White Question has reasserted itself in the black resistance to both the apartheid regime and its new constitutional proposals which were overwhelmingly adopted in November 1983 in a referendum by the white electorate.[28]

These proposals were the means whereby white power attempted to integrate Asians and "Coloureds" into its white supremacist structures. They constituted, along with the Riekert and Wiehahn commissions, what Stuart Hall has called in a different context a "formative strategy" of a ruling class confronting an "organic crisis."[29] The new constitution as well as the Riekert and Wiehahn commissions should be interpreted as the white ruling class's project to reorganize the state in an effort to diffuse the organic crisis and neutralize the "black threat."[30] In other words, this ruling class project was a response to the crisis; it consisted of "preventing the development of a revolutionary adversary by 'decapitating' its revolutionary potential."[31] Accordingly, the white ruling class project represents what Gramsci called a passive revolution. In fact, it expresses the white ruling class's search for a new hegemony in so far as this class attempts to relinquish its open and unabashed racism as its methods of governance to adopt a politics of co-optation and hegemonic de-racialization. The white ruling class seeks to assert is hegemony through universalizing its own corporate interests and ensuring that these could "become the interests of the . . . subordinate gropups."[32]

Hence, in order to preserve its domination, the white ruling class seeks to effect a passive revolution which goes beyond the promotion of its narrow and most immediate corporate interests.

The politics of "pure white supremacy" are slowly displaced by the politics of hegemonic de-racialization which maintains the structures of power fundamentally unchanged. This is precisely why the politics of hegemonic de-racialization should be viewed as a process of passive revolution.

Indeed, Gramsci's notion of passive revolution derives from Burkean conservatism which asserted that "society has to change in order to stay the same, i.e. to preserve its most essential features."[33] Accordingly, a passive revolution is a preemptive response from the ruling classes to the disorganized but potentially revolutionary demands of dominated classes. It is the specific peaceful means of survival of a ruling class in conditions of organic crisis. As Gramsci put it:

> A crisis occurs, sometimes lasting for decades. This exceptional duration means that incurable structural contradictions have revealed themselves. . . . and that, despite this, the political forces which are struggling to conserve and defend the existing structure itself are making every effort to cure them, within certain limits, and to overcome them. These incessant and persistent efforts . . . form the terrain of the "conjunctural," and it is upon this terrain that the forces of opposition organise.[34]

The terrain of the "conjunctural" however, has "no-far-reaching historical significance," despite its being the arena of immediate political and economic struggles.[35] Of much greater significance is the organic crisis which relates to a crisis of total structures and engenders what Stuart Hall has called the "formative efforts" of the ruling class.[36] These formative efforts, to paraphrase Hall, are an attempt to forge a new balance of forces and propel the emergence of new elements. They seek to put together a new "historical bloc" as well as new political configurations and philosophers. "Formative efforts involve thus a profound restructuring of the state and the ideological discourse which construct the crisis and represent it as it is "lived" as a practical reality. Consequently, new programs and policies pointing to a new result, a new sort of "settlement"—"within certain limits"—are required.[37] "These do not 'emerge': they have to be constructed. Political and ideological work is required to disarticulate old formations, and to rework their elements into new configurations."[38] The hegemonic de-racialization of South Africa embodies therefore the formative efforts of a ruling class confronting the organic crisis generated by the contradictions of white supremacy itself.

It would be wrong, however, to view such hegemonic de-racialization as a simple and easy process of reform. Indeed, this process is difficult and contradictory and it may ultimately fail miserably. Hegemonic de-racialization confronts not only the resistance of significant white sectors but it faces also the problems associated with the creation of a cooperative black bourgeoisie. Any successful passive revolution would have to be based on a strategy of black "embourgeoisement" which would be opposed in all likelihood by important blocks of the white population. As Sam Nolutshungu has remarked:

> In any project of black embourgeoisement it would be . . . the Afrikaner petty bourgeoisie and the state bourgeoisie which would be threatened with economic as well as political competition. If that project involved a significant sharing of state power with Blacks it would directly threaten the position not only of the petty bourgeoisie but also of the bureaucratic bourgeoisie itself.[39]

In addition to such white opposition, the managers of hegemonic de-racialization will be hard put to enlist a collaborating black elite capable of upholding and legitimizing the reformed structures of white supremacy. Post-Soweto African politics have on the one hand forced the white state to develop a strategy of passive revolution, and on the other, enhanced black resistance to this very strategy. Yet, it would be quite mistaken to ignore that passive revolution might well erect considerable structural and political constraints for the radical and revolutionary transformation of South Africa. Passive revolution may offer to some sectors of the African elites certain social and material advantages which may prove to be irresistible temptations to collaboration and gradualism. To recognize the significance of these temptations is not to deny the scope and radical nature of black resistance, but to point to both the obdurate limits to passive revolution and the difficulties and contradictions facing an African revolution.

It is this constrained environment which has moulded the shape of black opposition to hegemonic de-racialization. The opposition was led by the United Democratic Front (UDF) and the National Forum (NF), formed respectively in May and June 1983.[40] The UDF, rooted in the tradition of the ANC's Freedom Charter, is bent on mobilizing all anti-apartheid forces irrespective of their races. Its multiracial policy, however, has been vigorously attacked by the National Forum whose adherence to the ideology of the Black Consciousness Movement has implied eschewing alliances with whites. While both the UDF and NF have a few common leaders and members, the antagonism between the two is clear. Zinzi Mandela, a leading figure of the UDF and the daughter of Nelson Mandela, the historic but jailed leader of the ANC, condemned the NF as a group of "ideologically lost political bandits" who "diverted the struggle" because they failed to adhere to the multiracial principles of the Freedom Charter.[41]

The NF, however, identifying negatively the UDF as non-revolutionary "charterists," proclaimed in its *Manifesto of the Azanian People:*

> Our struggle for national liberation is directed against the system of racial capitalism which holds the people of Azania in bondage for the benefit of the small minority of white capitalists and their allies, the white workers and the reactionary sections of the black middle class. The struggle against apartheid is no more than the point of departure for our liberation efforts. Apartheid will be eradicated with the system of racial capitalism.[42]

The radicalism of the NF and AZAPO, however, has failed to eclipse the UDF which enjoys the larger following because of its call for a wider multiracial and non-ideological anti-apartheid front. Thus, despite its brave pronouncement that they have "become the vanguard of the people's struggle," AZAPO and its affiliated organizations have so far lacked the means and popular basis to constitute the dominant vehicle of the African revolution.

The African National Congress occupies that position of dominance.[43] Not surprisingly, when the youngsters of Soweto left South Africa in 1977 to prepare for their eventual military return they tended to come under the umbrella of the ANC. So what Kane-Berman has called the "exodus of the Graduates"[44] was the inevitable result of the youngsters' search for an organizational base, material resources, and international connections necessary for the transition to armed violence. Like their elders during the 1950's, this new generation of black youth became afflicted by an acute disenchantment with constitutional means of protest and the few political options that they entailed. It had finally opted for revolutionary violence. However, if the exodus of the graduates was motivated by the desire for guns, it did not automatically establish an ideological identity with the expatriate movement.

In fact on some important points, such as the role of whites in the struggle for liberation and the permissibility of African participation in Bantustan politics, contradictions existed. The unifying threads were opposition to apartheid and exploitation, the commitment to the armed struggle, and the hope for a socialistic and non-racist post-revolutionary South Africa. Thus, while it is possible to discover elements of convergence in Black Consciousness and ANC nationalism, it is clear that they were mutually distinct in several important ways.

The ANC regarded the Movement with sympathy, but with some reservations. For the ANC, Black Consciousness represented a positive movement with certain essential functions to perform. Black Consciousness, the ANC believed, was not only the bearer of important elements of a new culture, it had also a unifying influence on the oppressed ethnies; it served as an integral part of the revolutionary front. What is more, the ANC argued that the Black Consciousness Movement embodied the fundamental characteristics of an earlier period of the ANC's own history. In this sense Black Consciousness was a transitional social phenomenon which would inevitably integrate into the ideological and organizational fold of the ANC. As Oliver Tambo declared,

In a way we started from the point of black consciousness too, we formed the ANC from just Africans. . . . But we have not stayed there, we have developed to the position where we expect all the people in South Africa to form part of the movement for the transformation of the social, political and economic situation. Black consciousness, looked at from this point of view, is thus a phase in the struggle. It is not outside the struggle for human rights—on the contrary—it grows into the mainstream which has been set by the African National Congress.[45]

So, while the Black Consciousness Movement was part of a revolutionary tradition, its intellectual autonomy was denied and its originality contested. This perception is misleading even if it contains some elements of truth. The intellectual originality of Black Consciousness is valid, as was observed in the preceding chapters, even though many of its thematic expressions bear a close resemblance to those of the Africanist period of the ANC. Moreover, the extent of this originality can be found in some pronouncements of the ANC itself. In fact, during the early and mid-1970's the language and ideology of the ANC tended to swing increasingly towards the basic tenets of Black Consciousness.

Furthermore, it would not be too far fetched to suggest that it is the rise of Black Consciousness which precipitated the "national Africanist"[46] breakaway from the ANC in 1976. This break-away may be seen as part of, or at least intimately connected to, a reactionary interpretation of the Black Consciousness Movement. In this respect, the eight national Africanists who were expelled from the ANC may have thought that a general attack on the multiracial character and communist connections of the ANC would have secured them the leadership of a 'third force' comprising the bulk of the Black Consciousness Movement. It is therefore not surprising that their main arguments against the ANC centered upon its white membership and its alleged subjugation to the dictate of "white petty-bourgeois communism." The ANC, they declared, had "fallen under the complete domination of a small clique loyal to the White-led South African Communist Party,"[47] which had "nothing but disdain for the African people whom they regard as inferior in the same way the Vorster regime regards Africans as children who cannot be trusted with determining their own future."[48]

It is difficult not to link this virulent attack on white participation in the revolutionary process to the Black Consciousness slogan: "Black man you are on your own." And it is even more difficult not to see in this superficial ideological convergence an opportunist attempt to divert the Black Consciousness Movement to the national Africanist cause.

Be that as it may, the question of white participation in the revolutionary movement has always been problematic and it remains uncertain whether it has been resolved. Despite the optimistic assurances of Alfred Nzo, according to whom such participation created only transitory difficulties and even "resulted in a new level of enthusiasm,"[49] the "white question" remains an emotional and divisive issue.

It is this issue of white involvement in the liberation movement that made the ANC suspicious of the ultimate aims of Black Consciousness. The ambivalence with which the ANC regarded the Movement was well summed up in a 1973 editorial of Sechaba:

> . . . at this stage, while we must accept the revolutionary interpretation of Black Consciousness, we must at the same time, guard against and oppose, any manifestation of reactionary nationalistic or chauvinistic tendencies that may arise in the future.[50]

Hence, for the ANC, Janus-faced Black Consciousness contained not just elements of a progressive and revolutionary nationalism, but also tendencies for a degeneration into black jingoism. It was essential to harness its progressive potential and curb its chauvinistic undercurrents.

From the viewpoint of the ANC there were still further reservations. While the Black Consciousness Movement unleashed a counter-hegemonic force that effectively activated a black revolutionary identity, it was incapable by itself of making the necessary transition to revolutionary warfare. According to the ANC:

> To be effective, a break with the cultural and spiritual mode that the enemy has imposed on us cannot but be sharp and violent. . . . The assertion of the revolutionary identity of the oppressed black peoples is therefore not an end in itself. It can be a vital force of the revolutionary action involving the masses of the people, for it is in struggle, in the actual physical confrontation with the enemy that the people gain a lasting confidence in their own strength and in the inevitability of final victory—it is through action that the people acquire true psychological emancipation.[51]

But if it is in the actual physical confrontation with the enemy that the people gain a lasting confidence in their own strength, it became imperative to define and to develop a strategy towards the "enemy." Here again the "white question" inevitably came to the fore. If the primary objective of the revolution is the overthrow of white supremacy, is the white ethnie as a whole the enemy? Should this ethnie be portrayed as a monolithic and indivisible counter-revolutionary force? Can the initiation of revolutionary action induce a breakdown in its unity?

While the advocates of Black Consciousness recognized that the white ethnie was not a monolith, they held the belief that its small liberal-democratic fringe was at best irrelevant and at worst an obstacle to revolution. Thus, the white ethnie as a whole had to be condemned to prevent it from diluting the revolutionary will of the black masses. Any possible alliance with its liberal faction had to be resisted, and the most that could be expected from such a white faction was its neutrality during the struggle. Hence, to seek a unity with white forces, however well meaning they may be, constituted an exercise in futility.

For the ANC, on the contrary, the success of the revolution presupposed the breakdown of white unity. To divide the white bloc into feuding factions was an essential task since it would precipitate the disintegration of the racist political system. Moreover, the real alternative raised by a breakdown of white unity was indeed that of integrating revolutionary whites into the liberation movement to modify the traditional and popular black conviction that all whites were racist and reactionary subjects. Thus, in 1973 the ANC put forward the following thesis:

As the struggle intensifies, and the polarisation of forces and their confrontation sharpens, the question of dividing the enemy and of isolating the most stubborn racist elements and those most consistently interested in the continued existence of the white supremacist state, whatever the cost, will assume greater significance. It is therefore essential that, without compromising the unity of the oppressed peoples, who are the main motive force of the revolution, we must evince enough tactical flexibility to take whatever opportunity arises to bring over to our side, or neutralize, such forces as we can, from among the ranks of the enemy's social base: the whites.[52]

In political terms, this meant that the ANC was actively pursuing a strategy of broad popular alliances. While it relied primarily on the contribution of the black oppressed majority, it sought to draw into its fold the progressive white faction. Now, it is clear that the stress placed on the broadening of the unity of the liberation movement carried within it the seeds of a "middle-class solution."[53] The possibility of such a solution was most evident in the Bantustan policy followed by the ANC.

In opposition to the Black Consciousness Movement which refused to make any agreement—even a tactical one—with the black ruling classes of the Bantustans, the ANC, while completely dismissing the scheme of separate development, saw in these classes a potential ally in the struggle against apartheid. The idea behind such a strategy was to link these ruling classes to the liberation movement in order to radicalize them and use their legal status to further the internal erosion of the racist political system.[54]

The creation of such linkages with apparently reactionary black groups was for the ANC a fundamental strategic task, one that was motivated by the primacy of what was defined as "unity in action." Questioned on the views held by the ANC on organizations such as Chief Gatsha Buthelezi's Inkatha,[55] and AZAPO, Oliver Tambo replied:

The African National Congress is continuously encouraging our people to organise themselves into all manner of formations to continue the struggle and to raise the level of confrontation. We, therefore, welcome the emergence of all organisations that seek to

> unite our people in the struggle against the fascist dictatorship. . . .
> [what] is of decisive importance is unity in action—action which
> draws the masses of the people into struggle against White minority
> domination and exploitation. . . . There can be no question of
> agreements with anybody outside of this framework.[56]

Thus the ANC's concept of unity in action centers upon the building of popular coalitions which transcend an exclusive revolutionary-socialist basis and appeal to the emotionally-laden, nationalist sentiment as a catalyst to the radicalization and mobilization of the masses. The question, of course, is how can such unity in action radicalize and mobilize the masses if its articulation is placed in any way under the tutelage of the ruling classes of the Bantustans? In view of the social interests and activities of these classes, one need not be an inveterate skeptic to question the likelihood of their commitment to the radicalization and mobilization of the masses.

The concept of unity in action embraces two struggles that are inherent in the revolutionary process—the destruction of the white supremacist system, and the socialist transformation of the inherited political economy. While these struggles are not contradictory and are in fact interwoven, their complete resolution is inextricably linked to the dominance and guidance achieved by proletarian consciousness and leadership in the unity in action. Since the destruction of the racist social order requires neither a socialist commitment nor the development of a proletarian hegemony, unity in action may easily become the tool of a petty bourgeois alternative. Unity in action is truly revolutionary only when it specifically links the struggle against racism to the struggle for socialism. Such a specific linkage cannot develop by itself; it has to originate in the painful processes of guerrilla warfare.

To expect from the petty bourgeois leadership a voluntary and spontaneous renunciation of its capitalist predispositions, and its corresponding metamorphosis into a socialist vanguard, is to believe that all that is needed is to adopt the rhetoric and phraseology of the Marxist language. The petty bourgeoisie is only likely to become socialist when it is forced to do so by the powerful pressures of an armed proletarian and peasant mass, and even this may prove insufficient. In this perspective Joe Slovo, one of the major theorists of the ANC, was quite right to argue that,

> The inevitable future victory will undoubtedly owe a great deal to the persistence of the liberation movement's turn to a policy of armed struggle. Had it failed to act at all, it would have disappeared as a viable agency for change. Without actions which continued to emphasize that force is vital in the struggle for people's power, it would have left the field clear for a more ready acceptance at home and abroad of a reformist rather than a revolutionary solution.[57]

It is also quite clear that if the ANC had not kept alive the prospects of an armed alternative, it would have been incapable of providing a new political basis for the further radicalization of the youngsters of the Black Consciousness Movement. For, despite the fact that the underground of the ANC was not directly responsible for the Soweto uprisings, it assumed an effective if limited role in the organization of the students. According to the secretary-general of the South African Students Movement, Tebello Motapanyane:

> In 1974 small organised groups were created which used to meet in secret places. Those cells were concentrated mostly in Soweto, Durban and so on. To be specific and to be direct: they were initiated by the national liberation movement, that is, the ANC. . . . They were formed by the ANC. We in SASM did not actually think of forming such things. We were operating legally and tried to keep SASM as a broad legal organization. But some of us listened to our elders from the ANC when they said we needed more than just mass legal organizations. Hence we founded these underground cells.[58]

While the extent of its impact remains a matter of controversy, the ANC was definitely known and active in student circles during the mid-1970's. The claims made by Tsietsi Mashinini, a former President of the Soweto Students Representative Council, that the ANC "has hardly mobilised an army to bring about change"[59] and that is was "extinct internally,"[60] are clearly belied by the facts. For, not only did the ANC distribute leaflets and newspapers, it was also gradually reestablishing a network of cells throughout the country.[61] Mosima Sexwale, a former student at Orlando West High School, provided a more accurate version of events in his statement from the dock:

> Throughout the universities and high schools of South Africa, the South African Students' Organization and its . . . high-school equivalent, the South African Students' Movement, were very active in conducting meetings to preach the philosophy of black consciousness. . . . The oldest and largest political organisation was the African National Congress. There were many former members living in the townships and the ANC was a common topic of discussion. . . .[62]

Nevertheless, it remains true as the ANC itself acknowledged that its "voice [was] still relatively weak."[63] While its presence was felt it was not yet the hegemonic internal force of the black revolution. The ANC's incapacity to guide and control the Soweto uprisings was symptomatic of its revolutionary and organizational limitations.

Similarly, the Black Consciousness Movement, insofar as it was embodied in black communalism, represented an incomplete revolutionary formulation in terms of its political and economic theorizations. It is not that these theorizations were completely absent, but rather that their content exhibited serious lacunae and significant omissions. The result is that apart from the obvious condemnation of the economic ramifications of apartheid, there was very little sustained analysis on the South African political economy. This lack of serious theorizations on politics and economics was a marked feature of the young leadership of the Movement. There were no major efforts at elucidating the social order that would spring from what was described as the "certainty of revolutionary victory." The scale and forms of the transformation of the white supremacist order into a democratic and socialist system presented a formidable theoretical challenge from which the Black Consciousness Movement tended to shrink.

In this perspective the Black Consciousness Movement had yet to reach the full stage of revolutionary and socialist radicalization. For while it decisively rejected the ideological hegemony of the white ethnie and the liberal encomium to incrementalist reforms, it cannot be said that its socialist commitment was grounded in a coherent and detailed analysis of South African capitalism nor that it seriously considered the problems represented by the promised transition to African communalism. It is true that the Black Consciousness Movement developed a profound sense of moral outrage at capitalist exploitation, but Black Communalism did not represent a firm and comprehensive socialist program.

While this program entailed a profound transformation of South African capitalism and a redistribution of wealth between classes and races, it was not incompatible with the continued existence of capitalist relations of production. In fact, this program did not depart significantly from what has been called "modern capitalism" or "welfare state": *it did not necessarily* go beyond the contemporary liberal preoccupation with social welfare and equalization of opportunities.[64] Hence, it would appear that Black Communalism, in spite of its demands for the nationalization of banks and mining conglomerates and the establishment of communal agricultural cooperatives, represented programs of far-reaching reforms—but not of total structural transformations of the existing political and economic institutions.

Moreover, except for vague notions of workers' control of industry and a Marxist phraseology, little was said about the transition to socialism. In fact, the Black Consciousness Movement did not get very far in the development and presentation of a systematic theory of South African capitalism and African Communalism. It had neither the time during its short period of legal existence nor the environmental facilities during conditions of state repression to embark on a well-defined economic program for the transition to African socialism. It had also to contend with its relative isolation from the popular manifestations of black revolts. Such an isolation contributed to the absence of an organic linkage between leaders and masses and this in turn lessened the urgency for radical and comprehensive theorizations on social and economic policies.

However, it would be quite wrong to dismiss the Black Consciousness Movement as reformist petty bourgeois coalitions. For if it suffered from a "crisis of theory" it certainly did not accept the status quo nor the capitalist order. In fact, it developed a strong socialist undercurrent, however vague, confused, and immature it may have been. Its commitment to communalism and sharing, to equality and cooperation, and to democracy and fraternity, while not necessarily revolutionary in itself, is an essential and integral part of a socialist transformation of society. Furthermore, the decision to embark on guerrilla warfare in the aftermath of the bannings of 1977 and to join the expatriate movement—in particular the African National Congress—had not just military and violent implications; it contributed also to the radicalization of the liberation movement and to a growing revolutionary practice from which may emerge serious programmatic theorizations and alternative forms of popular power.

Hence, recognition that the Black Consciousness Movement was handicapped by its failure to produce a comprehensive theory of revolutionary transformations does not mean that this failure is irreversible and permanent. In fact, the trauma and ugliness of guerrilla warfare may represent the necessary first step in the development of a more rigorous knowledge of South African capitalism and a more elaborate program on the transition to African socialism. The ushering in of revolutionary violence may also determine the extent and scope of the process of class formation, and whether this process will propel to the fore a black elite of honorary whites bent on preserving the status quo.

The Black Consciousness Movement's determinate rejection of collaboration with those elements participating in and associated with the structures of separate development appears to be a correct and revolutionary position. Black Consciousness has identified the enemy as not only the white minority, but also as the emerging African elite. Such an identification should become clearer as the revolutionary struggle unfolds and as the involvement of the Movement and the ANC in the practical activities and collective struggles of the black masses increases.

Thus, it is evident that the Black Consciousness Movement had not reached the crucial point of junction between leaders and masses, and between theory and practice. But it is equally evident that the unfolding revolutionary struggle has the potential for materializing such a junction. This unfolding revolutionary struggle has already sapped the moral and political underpinnings of the white supremacist order. It has introduced profound contradictions into the racist power structure which has been stripped of its aura of legitimacy and authority. This power structure is no longer clothed by its traditional, protective, ideological cuirass; the old colonial consciousness which allowed the rule of racism to endure without the persistent, overt, and massive use of physical violence has progressively vanished.

The general breakdown of white cultural and ideological hegemony has set the stage for the black revolution. During this interregnum, the legalization of state violence is a sign of the powers of white supremacy—and the symptom of its impending dissolution. Indeed, such legalization of state violence mirrors the growing strength of black resistance and its increasing capacity to strain the overall system of race domination.[65] Thus, as the International Defense and Aid Fund has remarked:

> Military force and control is now at the centre of the strategy to preserve apartheid, rather than being one aspect among several. The strength of the [South African Defense Forces (SADF)] has been hugely increased, with a dramatic growth in conscripted manpower and a defence budget which rose from R472 million in 1973 to R1,899 million in 1978. The domestic arms industry has been rapidly expanded, and measures have been introduced to integrate the civilian economy into the war effort. What can best be described as a "war psychosis" is in the process of being created amongst the white civilian population, with other political and economic goals being subordinated to the needs and demands of the Defence Force.
>
> Most significantly, perhaps, military objectives and policy have been integrated to a far greater extent than ever before into the machinery of government. The SADF is today no longer seen as a necessary tool of government, but is instead an increasingly powerful force within the government itself. South Africa is now a military state, armed to defend the interests of the white minority against the desires of the people for a free, unified and non-racial society.[66]

The road to majority rule, let alone to a socialist South Africa, will be extremely difficult and risky. The problem of creating a solid and effective corps of guerrillas; the impressive might of the white state and its determination to use it against any black challenge; the as yet immature and confused theory of African communalism; the absence of programmatic economic thinking; and the process of class formation and "embourgeoisement" taking place within the African ethnie, are all reminders that African opposition and resistance to white supremacy could ultimately end in disappointment and defeat.

The fact that the Black Consciousness Movement has shown extreme confidence in the triumph of its cause and adopted an increasingly Marxian phraseology cannot be taken as evidence that its seizure of power in conjunction with the other liberation movements and in particular the ANC is inevitable, nor that such a seizure of power will make automatic the transition to a democratic socialism. But what is certain is that leaders and militants of the liberation movement have a considerable opportunity to secure a massive transformation of the political economy of South Africa. They have a considerable opportunity to break the chain of exploitation which has hitherto bound black South Africans to conditions of misery and deprivation. The future is theirs; what they will make of it remains uncertain.

The uncertainty stems not only from the vicissitudes of guerrilla warfare but also from the programmatic escapism of the liberation movements. The absence of clear theorizations on the transformation of the existing economic and political systems blurs the future direction and policies of a de-racialized, liberated South Africa, and represents a serious handicap to the revolutionary process itself. It appears that when critical thinking is most necessary, the liberation movement has become bogged down in a relative theoretical complacency. Instead of launching analytical efforts which would open new avenues for the revolutionary transformation of the existing capitalist reality, it goes on seeking old nostrums and reviving past doctrines. While it is true that the Black Consciousness Movement embodied a new political vision of African liberation, it was deeply influenced by previous conditions and struggles. Thus, despite the development of a new social and economic environment, the Black Consciousness Movement failed, for a variety of reasons such as those already mentioned and many others as well, to embark on serious programmatic thinking.

The programmatic escapism of Black Consciousness implies, however, neither moderation nor gradualism. In fact, the Black Consciousness Movement developed a strong anti-capitalist ethos; denouncing the individualistic tendencies of the bourgeois order, it proposed, however vaguely and confusedly, a communalism which favored the economic needs of the lower income groups and what was thought to be the inherent brotherhood of African lifestyles. While these demands and hopes were not conclusive socialist commitments, they were significant. Hence, a profound desire for change, if not total change, permeated the consciousness of the youngsters of Soweto. However, this desire for change had yet to become theoretical and programmatic. Similarly, instead of hard-headed reasoning on racist and capitalist exploitation, there was moral outrage; and this, however gratifying emotionally, did not go far beyond rhetorical sloganizing.

The commitment to revolutionary violence had yet to be matched by a clear analytical understanding of the present and a comprehensive vision of the future. The absence of theoretical thinking in the liberation movement may in fact be related to its conviction of ultimate victory which tended to make theory itself redundant: If the emancipation of black people was assured, and if the certainty of the triumph of the cause of liberation was unquestionable, then the search for a rigorous theory of the African revolution could be dismissed. This unshakable faith in ultimate victory distracted the Black Consciousness Movement from the realities of the capitalist economy and obscured the need for programmatic analyses, though it probably constituted an essential and necessary element for generating the human energy required for any revolutionary effort.

The Black Consciousness Movement had yet to develop the political unity between theory and practice without which the major structural transformation of society is impossible. For, as Amilcar Cabral, the late revolutionary leader of Guinea-Bissau, observed, "If it is true that a revolution can fail, even though it be nurtured on perfectly conceived theories, nobody has yet successfully practiced revolution without a revolutionary theory."[67] Only when this is well realized by black South Africans can their seizure of political power usher in a more egalitarian and democratic social order. Only then will the rhetoric of socialism and human brotherhood have a chance to materialize.

NOTES

Chapter I

1. The relationship between class and forms of nationalist protests is analyzed in Brian Willan, "The 'Gift of the Century': Solomon Plaatje, De Beers and the Old Kimberley Tram Shed, 1918-1919," in *The Societies of Southern Africa in the 19th and 20th Centuries*, 8, 22 (University of London Institute of Commonwealth Studies, 1978), pp. 77-93. See also Martin Legassick, "Records of Protest and Challenge," *Journal of African History*, 20, 3 (1979), pp. 451-455. Hereafter cited as: Legassick, *Protest;* Shula Marks, "The Ambiguities of Dependence: John L. Dube of Natal," *Journal of Southern African Studies*, I, 2 (April 1975), pp. 162-180; and Paul Rich, "African Politics and the Cape African Franchise, 1926-1936," in *The Societies of Southern Africa in the 19th and 20th Centuries*, 9, 24 (University of London Institute of Commonwealth Studies, 1978), pp. 127-136. Hereafter cited as: Rich, *African Politics.*

2. T. D. Ranger, "Connexions Between 'Primary Resistance' Movements and Modern Mass Nationalism in East and Central Africa: II," *Journal of African History*, IX, 4 (1968), p. 631. Hereafter cited as Ranger, *Connexions: II.* See also Charles Van Onselen, "South Africa's Lumpen-Proletarian Army: 'Umkosi Wa Ntaba'—'The Regiment of the Hills', 1890-1920," *The Societies of Southern Africa in the 19th and 20th Centuries*, 7, 21 (University of London Institute of Commonwealth Studies, 1977), pp. 77-103; and Shula Marks, *Reluctant Rebellion: The 1906-8 Disturbances in Natal* (Oxford: Oxford University Press, 1970), p. XX.

3. See Peter Walshe, *The Rise of African Nationalism* (Berkeley: University of California Press, 1971). Hereafter cited as: Walshe, *African Nationalism.* See also, Gail M. Gerhart, *Black Power in South Africa* (Berkeley: University of California Press, 1978), pp. 85-123. Hereafter cited as: Gerhart, *Black Power.*

4. Gerhart, *Black Power,* pp. 124-251.

5. See Note 1.

6. Frantz Fanon, *Black Skins, White Masks* (New York: Grove Press, 1967).

7. Gerhart, *Black Power,* pp. 45-84; Walshe, *African Nationalism,* pp. 349-361.

8. Gerhart, *Black Power,* pp. 173-235.

9. Anton Lembede, "Policy of the Congress Youth League," in *From Protest to Challenge,* Vol. II, ed. Thomas Karis and Gwendolen M. Carter (Stanford: Hoover Institution Press, 1973), p. 318. Hereafter cited as: Lembede, *Policy.* See also Gerhart, *Black Power,* pp. 45-84.

149

10. See Gerhart, *Black Power,* p. 62.

11. In its Manifesto, CYL opposed European individualism arguing that it bred continual and deadly conflicts for Africans who were striving for ultimate unity and collective order. The African regarded the universe as:

> . . . one composite whole; an organic entity, progressively driving towards greater harmony and unity whose individual parts exist merely as interdependent aspects of one whole realizing their fullest life in the corporate life where communal contentment is the absolute measure of values. His philosophy of life strives towards unity and aggregation; towards greater social responsibility. ("Congress Youth League Manifesto," in *From Protest to Challenge,* Vol. II, p. 301. Hereafter cited as: *CYL Manifesto.*)

See also, Gerhart, *Black Power,* pp. 61–62.

12. *Ibid.*

13. Walshe, *African Nationalism,* pp. 355–369.

14. Lembede, *Policy,* p. 318.

15. Gerhart, *Black Power,* pp. 317–319; Walshe, *African Nationalism,* p. 34.

16. Walshe, *African Nationalism,* p. 121.

17. E. P. Thompson, *The Making of the English Working Class* (New York: Vintage Books, 1966), p. 939.

18. H. J. and R. E. Simons, *Class and Colour in South Africa, 1850–1950* (Baltimore: Penguine Books, 1969), pp. 428–429. Hereafter cited as: Simons, *Class.* See also Note 1.

19. Walshe, *African Nationalism,* p. 121.

20. Simons, *Class,* p. 429.

21. Brian Bunting, *The Rise of the South African Reich* (Baltimore: Penguin Books, 1969). Hereafter cited as: Bunting, *Reich.*

22. Walshe, *African Nationalism,* pp. 327–401.

23. "Programme of Action," in *From Protest to Challenge,* Vol. II, pp. 337–339. Hereafter cited as: *Programme of Action.* See also Walshe, *African Nationalism,* pp. 290–294.

24. "Africans' Claims," in *From Protest to Challenge, Vol. II,* pp. 209–223. Hereafter cited as: *Claims.* See also Walshe, *African Nationalism,* pp. 271–279.

25. *Programme of Action,* p. 337.

26. Walshe, *African Nationalism,* p. 354.

27. Basil Davidson, *Let Freedom Come* (Boston: Atlantic Monthly Press Book, 1978), p. 202. Hereafter cited as: Davidson, *Freedom.*

28. See Walshe, *African Nationalism,* pp. 355–369.

29. Joe Matthews cited as quoted in Walshe, *African Nationalism,* p. 349.

30. *Ibid.,* p. 361.

31. *Ibid.*

32. *Ibid.,* pp. 379–405.

33. *Ibid.,* p. 403.

34. For a brief analysis of the African Democratic Party, the Non-European Movement, and the All-African Convention see Thomas Karis, "Moderation and Militancy, 1937–1949," in *From Protest to Challenge, Vol. II,* pp. 107–114. Hereafter cited as: Karis, *Moderation.*

35. See Simons, *Class,* pp. 570–578.

36. The ANC, the South African Indian Congress, the African People's Organization, and the Communist Party staged a one-day strike in protest against the Act

on June 26, 1950. This protest ended in failure, but June 26 became known as Freedom Day. In the words of Brian Bunting, the Act "formed the spearhead of the Nationalist attack on the civil liberties of all sections of the population, communist and non-communist alike." Bunting, *Reich,* p. 199. For more details on the consequences of this Act see, Bunting, *Reich,* pp. 198–201.

37. "Report of the Joint Planning Council of the ANC and the South African Congress," in *From Protest to Challenge, Vol. II,* p. 459. Hereafter cited as: *Joint Planning.*

38. Dr. J. S. Moroka, "Presidential Address," in *From Protest to Challenge, Vol. II,* p. 459. Hereafter cited as: *Joint Planning.*

39. Dr. S. M. Molema, "Opening Address," in *From Protest to Challenge, Vol. II,* pp. 477–482.

40. The Gandhian ethic of Satyagraha is studied and contrasted to the African concept of peaceful resistance in Leo Kuper, *Passive Resistance in South Africa* (New Haven: Yale University Press, 1957), pp. 72–94. Hereafter cited as: Kuper, *Passive Resistance.*

41. *Joint Planning,* pp. 460–461.

42. *Ibid.,* p. 464.

43. *Ibid.,* p. 465.

44. See Kuper, *Passive Resistance,* pp. 104–105.

45. *Joint Planning,* p. 462.

46. Julius Lewin, *Politics and Law in South Africa* (London: Merlin Press, 1963), p. 113.

47. This Act empowered the government to rule by decree and to declare a state of emergency.

48. This Act provided for very severe penalties for any offense "by way of protest or in support of any campaign against any law." See Thomas Karis, "The Congress Movement, 1953–1956," in *From Protest to Challenge, Vol. III,* ed. Thomas Karis, Gwendolen M. Carter and Gail Gerhart (Stanford: Hoover Institution Press, 1977), p. 6. Hereafter cited as: Karis, *Congress.*

49. Nelson R. Mandela, "No Easy Walk to Freedom," in *From Protest to Challenge, Vol. II,* p. 108. Hereafter cited as: Mandela, *Freedom.*

50. *Ibid.,* p. 112.

51. "Report of the National Executive Committee," in *From Protest to Challenge, Vol. III,* pp. 158–159. Hereafter cited as: *Report of NEC.*

52. See Karis, *Congress,* pp. 24–29.

53. *Ibid.,* pp. 29–35.

54. Karis, *Congress,* p. 30.

55. The South African Congress of Trade Unions (SACTU), formed in 1954, collaborated closely with the Congress Alliance. Its left wing tendencies contributed to the radicalization of the alliance and the Freedom Charter's nationalization plank.

56. Jordan Ngubane, the principal African liberal figure, broke with the ANC to join the Liberal Party because he saw communist influence behind the Freedom Charter. He expressed well the liberal hysteria over communism when he contended that the Charter's ultimate goal was "to condition the African people for the purpose of accepting communism via the back door." Quoted as cited in Karis, *Congress,* p. 64.

57. "Freedom Charter," in *From Protest to Challenge, Vol. III,* p. 205. Hereafter cited as: *Freedom Charter.*

58. *Ibid.,* pp. 206–208.

59. The Charter represented for Mandela "a revolutionary document precisely because the changes it envisages cannot be won without breaking up the economic and political set-up of present South Africa." Mandela, "In our Lifetime," in *From Protest to Challenge, Vol. III,* p. 246. Hereafter cited as: Mandela, *Lifetime.*

60. *Ibid.,* p. 247.

61. Mandela, *Lifetime,* p. 247. My emphasis.

62. Davidson, *Freedom,* pp. 227–228.

63. Mandela, *Lifetime,* p. 245.

64. Robert Sobukwe, "Future of the Africanist Movement," in *From Protest to Challenge, Vol. III,* pp. 507–508.

65. Robert Sobukwe, "Opening Address," in *From Protest to Challenge, Vol. III,* pp. 512–516.

66. Joe Matthews, " 'Africanism' under the Microscope," in *From Protest to Challenge, Vol. III,* p. 541.

67. *Ibid.,* p. 540.

68. As quoted in Thomas Karis, "The Last Stage of Non-Violence, 1957–May 1961," in *From Protest to Challenge, Vol. III,* pp. 345–346. Hereafter cited as: Karis, *The Last Stage.*

69. *Ibid.,* p. 346.

70. *Ibid.,* p. 347.

71. *Ibid.,* p. 348.

72. The modernization and development of the police apparatus are analyzed in Albie Sachs, *Justice in South Africa* (Berkeley: University of California Press, 1973), pp. 239–244; and in his article, "The Instruments of Domination in South Africa," in *Change in Contemporary South Africa,* ed. Leonard Thompson and Jeffrey Butler (Berkeley: University of California Press, 1975), pp. 223–249.

73. Robert Sobukwe, "Final Instructions," in *From Protest to Challenge, Vol. III,* p. 569.

74. Robert Sobukwe, "Press Release: Call for Positive Action," in *From Protest to Challenge, Vol. III,* p. 567. My emphasis.

75. *Ibid.*

76. Karis, *The Last Stage,* p. 332.

77. Cited as quoted in Thomas Karis, Gwendolyn M. Carter and Gail Gerhart, *From Protest to Challenge, Vol. III,* p. 749. Hereafter cited as: Karis, Carter and Gerhart: *Protest.*

78. As we will see, however, this conception of the "primacy of politics" was still embryonic. It suffered from a fatal flaw: it failed to bridge the gap between the leadership and the masses.

79. Arthur Daniel, "Radical Resistance to Minority Rule in South Africa: 1906–1965," (unpublished doctoral dissertation, State University of New York at Buffalo, 1975), pp. 355–361. Hereafter cited as: Daniel, *Radical Resistance.*

80. Frantz Fanon, *The Wretched of the Earth* (New York: Grove Press, 1968), p. 33.

81. Karis, Carter and Gerhart, *Protest,* p. 671.

82. Daniel, *Radical Resistance,* pp. 332–337 and pp. 355–361.

83. Karis, Carter and Gerhart, *Protest,* p. 750.

84. Bram Fischer, cited as quoted in *The Sun Will Rise,* ed. Mary Benson (London: International and Aid Fund, 1976), p. 46. Hereafter cited as: Benson, *The Sun.*

85. Ben Turok, "South Africa: The Search for a Strategy," in *The Socialist Register 1973,* ed. Ralph Miliband and John Saville (London: The Merlin Press, 1974), p. 361. Hereafter cited as: Turok, *A Strategy.*

86. When the police raided the Rivonia farm, Sisulu was meeting with Govan Mbeki, Raymond Mhlaba, Ahmed Kathrada, Lionel Bernstein and Bob Hepple. These six figures of the resistance movement were later joined by Mandela, Andrew Mlangeni, Elias Motsoaledi and others in the "Rivonia Trial."

87. Ben Turok, "South Africa: The Violent Alternative," in *The Socialist Register 1972,* ed. Ralph Miliband and John Saville (London: The Merlin Press, 1972), pp. 275–276. Hereafter cited as: Turok, *The Violent Alternative.*

88. Karis, Carter and Gerhart, *Protest,* pp. 649–651.

89. Karis, Carter and Gerhart, *Protest,* pp. 707–711.

90. *Ibid.,* p. 799.

91. A liberal splinter group created the African Resistance Movement (ARM) as a military alternative to peaceful protest. ARM was not affiliated with the Liberal Party; it was the creation of a small group of more radical liberals. For further details see Daniel, *Radical Resistance,* pp. 369–375.

92. Ted Honderich, *Violence for Equality* (Harmondsworth: Penguin Books, 1980), pp. 170–197.

93. Karis, Carter and Gerhart, *Protest,* p. 639.

94. *Ibid.,* p. 640.

95. Turok, *A Strategy,* p. 352.

96. This view is best expressed in Edward Feit, *Urban Revolt in South Africa 1960–1964* (Evanston: Northwestern, 1971).

97. Karis, Carter and Gerhart, *Protest,* p. 789.

98. *Ibid.,* p. 790.

99. *Ibid.,* p. 787.

100. *Ibid.,* p. 788.

101. See Bunting, *Reich,* pp. 158–243.

102. Karis, Carter and Gerhart, *Protest,* p. 660.

103. Antonio Gramsci, *Selections From the Prison Notebooks* (London: Lawrence and Wishart, 1971), pp. 59, 106–120.

104. *Ibid.,* p. 59.

105. Walter L. Adamson, *Hegemony and Revolution* (Berkeley: University of California Press, 1980), p. 186.

106. Cited as quoted in Richard Leonard, *South Africa at War* (Westport: Lawrence Hill & Company, 1983), p. 200.

107. Heribert Adam and Hermann Giliomee, *Ethnic Power Mobilized* (New Haven: Yale University Press, 1979), pp. 133–134.

108. See John S. Saul and Stephen Gelb, *The Crisis in South Africa* (New York: Monthly Review Press, 1981), pp. 32–44. Hereafter cited as: Saul and Gelb, *The Crisis.* See also Sam C. Nolutshungu, *Changing South Africa, Political Considerations* (Manchester: Manchester University Press, 1982), pp. 75–115.

109. Saul and Gelb, *The Crisis,* p. 34.

110. International Defence and Aid Fund, *The Apartheid War Machine* (London: IDAF, 1980), p. 40.

Chapter II

1. Barrington Moore, Jr., *Injustice: The Social Basis of Obedience and Revolt* (New York: M. E. Sharpe, 1978), pp. 458–459.

2. Goran Therborn, *What Does the Ruling Class Do When it Rules?* London: New Left Review Editions, 1980), p. 172.

3. See Goran Therborn, *The Ideology of Power and the Power of Ideology* (London: New Left Editions, 1980). For the best criticism of the structuralism of "deterministic Marxism" as embodied in L. Althusser and his followers, see E. P. Thompson, *The Poverty of Theory and Other Essays* (New York: Monthly Review Press, 1978). In the context of South African studies it is such structural Marxism that has achieved dominance. This is not the place to go into a detailed analysis and criticism of this school, but suffice it to say that its most significant writings are the following: Frederick A. Johnstone, *Class, Race and Gold,* (London: Routledge and Kegan Paul, 1976); Harold Wolpe (ed.), *The Articulation of Modes of Production* (London: Routledge and Kegan Paul, 1980). See entries in the bibliography of this study on Frederick Johnstone, Harold Wolpe, Martin Legassick, Innes Duncan and Robert Davies.

4. The deterministic outlook of the structural-Marxian school resides in the notion that the capitalist mode of production in South Africa is a self-reproducing mode of production, and in fact a mode that cannot be changed. Thus, Johnstone declares:

> Far from undermining white supremacy, economic development is constantly re-enforcing it. Its power structure is continually strengthened by its own material output. In a circular process, the African workers produce the wealth and power which enable the whites to go on strengthening this structure of production which goes on producing the power which goes on strengthening the structure and so on. ("White Prosperity and White Supremacy In South Africa Today," *African Affairs,* 69, 275 (April 1970), p. 136.)

5. Eugene D. Genovese, *In Red and Black. Marxian Explorations in Southern and Afro American History* (New York: Pantheon Books, 1971), p. 43.

6. Oliver Cox, *Caste, Class & Race* (New York: Monthly Review Press, 1970), pp. 317–391.

7. Robert H. Davies, *Capital, State and White Labour in South Africa: 1900–1960,* (Atlantic Highlands: Humanities Press, 1979), pp. 364–365. Hereafter cited as: Davies, *Capital.*

8. This information is taken from Stanley B. Greenberg, "Economic Growth and Political Change: The South African Case," *The Journal of Modern African Studies,* Vol. 19, No. 4 (1981), pp. 678–691. Hereafter cited as: Greenberg, *Economic Growth.*

9. Foreign Policy Study Foundation, *South Africa: Time Running Out. The Report of the Study Commission on U.S. Policy Toward Southern Africa* (Berkeley: University of California Press, 1981), p. 133. Hereafter cited as: Study, *Time Running Out.*

10. Greenberg, *Economic Growth,* p. 680.

11. *Ibid.*

12. Study, *Time Running Out,* pp. 106–108.

13. Roger Southall, *South Africa's Transkei,* (New York: Monthly Review Press, 1983), pp. 219–220.

14. Dunbar Moodie, *The Rise of Afrikanerdom* (Berkeley: University of California Press, 1975). Hereafter cited as: Moodie, *Afrikanerdom.* The articles of Dan O'Meara are probably the most important and illuminating on the relationship between Afrikaner nationalism and the growth of Afrikaner capitalism: "The Afrikaner Broederbond, 1927–1948: Class Vanguard of Afrikaner Nationalism," *Journal of Southern African Studies,* 3, 2 (April 1977), pp. 156–186; "Analyzing Afrikaner Nationalism: the 'Christian-National' Assault on White Trade Unionism in South Africa, 1934–1948," *African Affairs,* 77, 306 (January, 1978), pp. 45–72; "The 1946 African Mine Workers' Strike and the Political Economy of South Africa," *The Journal of Commonwealth and Comparative Politics,* 13, 2 (July 1975), pp. 146–173. See also Heribert Adam and Hermann Giliomee, *Ethnic Power Mobilized* (New Haven: Yale University Press, 1979), pp. 83–127. Hereafter cited as: Adam and Giliomee, *Ethnic Power.*

15. *Ibid.*

16. The term 'ethnie' was first used by French anthropologists to describe a federation of tribes united by their common origin, common culture and common language. Usually this union was precipitated by military threats or/and natural disasters. 'Ethnie' has been used also by English-speaking social scientists to express the same notions. See Horace B. Davis, *Toward a Marxist Theory of Nationalism* (New York: Monthly Review Press, 1978), pp. 203–204. See also Anthony D. Smith, *Theories of Nationalism* (New York: Harper & Row Publishers, 1971), p. 162.

I will use the term 'ethnie' to describe the ethnic mobilization and "regroupment" of the Afrikaner population.

17. W. A. de Klerk, *The Puritans in Africa: A History of Afrikanerdom* (Harmondsworth: Penguin Books, 1976), pp. 280–286.

18. Cited as quoted in Moodie, *Afrikanderdom,* pp. 203–204.

19. Cited as quoted in Ralph Horwitz, *The Political Economy of South Africa* (New York: Praeger, 1967), pp. 301–302. The Commission acquired its name from its chairman, Col. Stallard, who paradoxically became identified as an enemy of Afrikanerdom because of his association with British causes and interests.

20. David Mason, "Industrialisation, Race and Class Conflict in South Africa: Towards a Sociological Resolution of a Reopened Debate," *Ethnic and Racial Studies,* 3, 2 (April 1980), p. 149.

21. See Davies, *Capital,* pp. 24–25.

22. See Trapido. "South Africa in a Comparative Study of Industrialism," *The Journal of Development Studies,* VII, 3 (April 1971), pp. 309–320. Also see Legassick: "The Dynamics of Modernization in South Africa," *Journal of African History,* III, 3 (August 1974), pp. 253–291; and "Legislation, Ideology and Economy in Post 1948 South Africa," *Journal of Southern African Studies,* I, 1 (October 1974), pp. 5–35.

23. Adam and Giliomee, *Ethnic Power,* pp. 178–179.

24. Richard Leonard, *South Africa at War* (Westport: Lawrence Hill and Company, 1983), pp. 161–221.

25. The concept of 'hegemony' is used here in the Gramscian tradition. See Antonio Gramsci, *Selections from the Prison Notebooks of Antonio Gramsci,* edited and translated by Quintin Hoare and Geoffrey Nowell Smith (London: Lawrence and Wishart, 1971). Hereafter cited as: Gramsci, *Selections.* See also Carl Boggs, *Gramsci's Marxism* (London: Pluto Press, 1976).

26. Karl Marx and Frederick Engels, *The German Ideology* (New York: International Publishers, 1969), p. 39.

27. These concessions are embodied in the proposals contained in the Riekert and Wiehahn commissions. These proposals are an attempt to resolve the "urban and labor questions" through the partial integration of the better-off segments of the black population into a modified structure of white privilege. An excellent analysis of these proposals is provided in: John S. Saul and Stephen Gelb, *The Crisis in South Africa: Class Defense, Class Revolution* (New York: Monthly Review Press, 1981), pp. 63–90.

28. Southall, Roger, C., "The Beneficiaries of Transkeian Independence," *The Journal of Modern African Studies*, Vol. 15, 1 (1977), pp. 1–23.

29. Immanuel Wallerstein, *The Capitalist World-Economy* (Cambridge: Cambridge University Press, 1979), p. 228.

30. By 'ethico-political' I mean that the political manifestations of Black Consciousness were inseparable from their attachment to the moral code of Black Theology. They expressed the transcendence of the 'ethical demand' and the responsibility of human beings for their choice and actions.

31. Gramsci, *Selections*, p. 367.

32. *Ibid.*, pp. 3–43.

33. *Ibid.*, p. 334.

34. By 'opposing' strata I mean that the interests of the different black social groups conflict but are not necessarily mutually exclusive. Conversely, 'antagonistic' strata implies that these interests are necessarily mutually exclusive, and that there are no grounds for a progressive alliance of classes. For a more detailed discussion of 'contradictions' see Mao Tse-Tung, *Four Essays on Philosophy* (Peking: Foreign Languages Press, 1968), pp. 23–110.

35. The term 'petty bourgeoisie' will be used interchangeably with 'elites,' 'middle classes,' or 'middle-strata.' What Marx had to say about the middle classes applies equally to our understanding of their role in contemporary South Africa:

> What (Ricardo) forgets to mention is the continual increase in numbers of the middle classes . . . situated midway between the workers on one side and the capitalist and landowner on the other. These middle classes rest with all their weight upon the working class and at the same time increase the social security and power of the upper class. (Translated in T. B. Bottomore and Maximilien Rubel, *Karl Marx: Selected Writings in Sociology and Social Philosophy* (New York: McGraw-Hill Book Company, 1964, pp. 190–191).

36. R. H. Tawney, *Equality* (New York: Capricorn Books, 1961), pp. 108–109.

37. Gwyn Williams, "The Concept of 'Egemonia' in the Thought of Antonio Gramsci: Some Notes on Interpretation," *Journal of the History of Ideas*, XXI, 4 (October–December 1960), p. 587. There are parallels between Gramsci's claims that a successful socialist revolution requires as a prerequisite the "cultural hegemony" of the proletariat, and Black Consciousness' belief that the liberation of the black necessitates their cultural emancipation. In this sense, Black Consciousness is "Gramscian."

38. Antonio Gramsci, quoted as cited in Guiseppe Fiori, *Antonio Gramsci: Life of a Revolutionary* (London: New Left Books, 1970), p. 103.

Chapter III

1. Martin Legassick, *The National Union of South African Students: Ethnic Cleavage and Ethnic Integration in the Universities,* (Los Angeles: African Studies Center, University of California, 1967), Occasional Paper Number 4, p. 6.

2. The "tribal colleges" were created in 1959 by the University Education Act. As Richard Rathbone explained:

> This act ended the last vestiges of serious inter-racial study of South Africa. It closed the relatively open English language-medium universities of Cape Town, Natal (at Durban and Pietermartizburg), Rhodes (as Grahamstown), and the Witwatersrand to what were then called non-whites. Up to 1959 blacks could and did study at those universities although facilities in particular social amenities, remained segregated. ("Student and Politics," *The Journal of Commonwealth and Comparative Politics,* XV, 2 (July, 1977), pp. 103–104.)

3. Martin Legassick and John Shingler, "South Africa," in *Students and Politics in Developing Nations,* ed. Donald K. Emmerson (New York: Frederick A. Praeger, 1968), p. 137.

4. *Ibid.,* p. 137.

5. Barney Pityana to SRC Presidents, National Student Organizations, Other Organizations, Overseas Organizations, 1970. South African Students' Organization, Durban, p. 1. Hereafter cited as: Pityana, *SASO.*

However, the role of UCM in the formation and development of the Black Consciousness Movement should not be overstated. As Colin Collins—the former general secretary of UCM—observed,

> My own conclusion is that black polarization (and black consciousness) would have taken place sooner or later had the UCM not existed. The necessary prerequisite conditions were all there. Maybe an organization of a somewhat different character would have emerged had the UCM not been created. . . . What animated those of us who initiated the UCM was a deep sense of social justice and a desire to have a more egalitarian society in South Africa. . . . The polarization strategy was a direct result of the black people themselves, discarding their own sense of inferiority; the encouragement that they received within the UCM was to "go to it" on their own. . . . The Black Consciousness Movement was created by young black leaders and by them alone." (In Colin Collins, "How it Really Happened," Unpublished Paper, 1979), pp. 13–14.)

6. The UCM was formally dissolved in 1972. The reasons given for the dissolution were the following:

> —that the UCM itself had over the past few years advocated the need for black-white polarization.
> —that the Methodist and Presbyterian churches had finally withdrawn their support from the UCM without giving their reasons fully and clearly to the UCM in spite of the avenues that have existed for that.
> —that the UCM has had to operate against increasing pressure from the government and power structures in the universities." (Cited as quoted in

Bennie Khoapa, "Youth and Student Organization," in *Black Review,* 1972, ed. Bennie Khoapa (Durban: Black Community Programmes, 1973), p. 188.)

7.   Ranwedzi Nengwekhulu, "The Meaning of Black Consciousness in the Struggle for Liberation in South Africa," *United Nations Center Against Apartheid,* Notes and Documents, 16/76 (July 1976), p. 7. Hereafter cited as: Nengwekhulu, *The Meaning of Black Consciousness.*

8.   Gail Gerhart, *Black Power in South Africa* (Berkeley: University of California Press, 1978), pp. 45–84. Hereafter cited as: Gerhart, *Black Power.* See also Peter Walshe, *The Rise of African Nationalism in South Africa: The African National Congress, 1912–1952* (Berkeley: University of California Press, 1971), pp. 349–360.

9.   Bengt Sundkler, *Bantu Prophets in South Africa,* 2nd ed. (London: Oxford University Press, 1961), pp. 306–307.

10.   By bourgeois cultic ethos I mean the attachment of "white" Christianity to the individualistic and even racist values of the prevailing capitalist order. It constitutes a conservative moral code which contributes to keeping things as they are. Salvation in this conception of Christianity is seen as the result of an exclusive devotion to spiritual and non-worldly aspects of life. The church in this perspective is to remain outside the historical struggles of human praxis.

11.   Gerhart, *Black Power,* p. 204.

12.   Contrary to the "Africanists," Black Consciousness sought the unity of all exploited groups irrespective of their ethnic background. The term 'black' included Indians and "Coloureds" as well as all Africans.

13.   The "students-as-such" position is the position adopted by students who are essentially concerned with their own academic environment and not with the social problems of the wider society.

14.   The term "non-white" was finally dropped in 1970 and replaced by the term "black." I will use the term black in this essay to characterize those people coming from the African, "Coloured" and Indian ethnies who adopted Black Consciousness.

15.   Steve Biko, *I Write What I Like,* ed. Aelred Stubbs (New York: Harper & Row, 1978), pp. 4–5. Hereafter cited as: Biko, *I Write.*

16.   Pityana, *SASO,* p. 3.

17.   *Ibid.,* p. 4.

18.   *Ibid.,* p. 3.

19.   "SASO Policy Manifesto," *SASO Newsletter,* 1, 3 (August 1971), pp. 10–11.

20.   S. M. Motsuenyane, "Black Consciousness and the Economic Position of the Black Man in South Africa," in *Black Renaissance, Papers from the Black Renaissance Convention,* ed. Thoahlane Thoahlane (Johannesburg: Ravan Press, 1975), p. 47.

21.   *Ibid.,* pp. 49–50.

22.   Adam Small, "Blackness versus Nihilism: Black Racism Rejected," in *The Challenge of Black Theology in South Africa,* ed. Basil Moore (Atlanta: John Knox Press, 1974), p. 11.

23.   Biko, *I Write,* pp. 29–30.

24.   Manas Buthelezi, "An African Theology or a Black Theology?" in *The Challenge of Black Theology in South Africa,* ed. Basil Moore (Atlanta: John Knox Press, 1974), p. 32. Hereafter cited as: Buthelezi, *African Theology.*

25.   Njabulo Ndebele, "Black Development," in *Black Viewpoint,* ed. Steve Biko (Durban: Spro-Cas, 1972), p. 26. Hereafter cited as: Ndebele, *Black Development.*

26. The most important works of these black Americans include: Stokley Carmichael and Charles Hamilton, *Black Power: The Politics of Liberation in America* (New York: Random House, 1967); Eldridge Cleaver, *Soul on Ice*, with an introduction by Maxwell Geismar (New York: McGraw Hill, 1967); Malcolm X, *The Autobiography of Malcolm X*, ed. Alex Haley (New York: Grove Press, 1965); James Cone, *Black Theology and Black Power* (New York: The Seabury Press, 1969). Hereafter cited as: Cone, *Black Theology*.

27. See Millard Arnold, "Introduction," in Steve Biko, *Black Consciousness in South Africa*, ed. Millard Arnold (New York: Vintage Books, 1979), p. XXVII.

28. Steve Biko, *Black Consciousness in South Africa*, ed. Millard Arnold (New York: Vintage Books, 1979), pp. 118–119. Hereafter cited as: Biko, *Black Consciousness*.

29. Biko, *I Write*, p. 49.

30. Bennie A. Khoapa, "The New Black," in *Black Viewpoint*, ed. Steve Biko (Durban: Spro-Cas, 1972), p. 64. Hereafter cited as: Khoapa, *The New Black*.

31. Biko, *I Write*, pp. 91–92.

32. Steve Biko, interview with Gail Gerhart, cited as quoted in Sam C. Nolutshungu, *Changing South Africa. Political Considerations* (Manchester: Manchester University Press, 1982), p. 158.

33. Karl Marx, "For a Ruthless Criticism of Everything Existing," in *The Marx-Engels Reader*, ed. Robert C. Tucker (New York: Norton & Company, 1972), p. 10.

34. "SASO Policy Manifesto," *SASO Newsletter*, 1, 3 (August 1971), p. 11.

35. Gerhart, *Black Power*, p. 270.

36. "SASO Policy Manifesto," *SASO Newsletter*, 1, 3 (August 1971), p. 11.

Chapter IV

1. Temba Sono was President of SASO between 1971 and 1973, but he was forced to resign when he declared at the Third General Council of SASO:

> The notion of a revolution is out . . . because it is too singular . . . too one dimensional . . . we have to move away from the aloof attitude of regarding Bantustans and other separate development bodies in negative light . . . we have to seek out people who differ with us . . . black and white whether they are security police [,] liberals [,] non-whites [,] etc. . . . .

The above quotation is contained in Sono's speech that forced his resignation. As far as I know this speech, "In Search of a Free and New Society," was never published. However, a copy exists at the Melville J. Herskovits Library of African Studies of Northwestern University.

For SASO's reaction to Sono's speech see "The Third General Students' Council—An Assessment," *SASO Newsletter*, 2, 4 (September/October 1972), pp. 13–15.

The students' unrest was provoked when Ongkopotse Ramothibi Tiro was expelled from the University of the North (Turfloop) for delivering a speech on Graduation Day (29th April, 1972), in which he condemned the concept of Bantu Education. Tiro's speech is reproduced as "Bantu Education," *South African Outlook*, 102, 1213/1214 (June/July 1972), pp. 99–102. Tiro was subsequently murdered—probably by the South African security police—in a parcel bomb blast in 1974 while he was exiled in Botswana. For further information on the students' unrest see *A Survey of Race*

Relations, 1972, compiled by Muriel Horrell, Dudley Horner, John Kane-Berman and Robin Margo (Johannesburg: South African Institute of Race Relations, 1973), pp. 386–396.

2.   Bennie Khoapa, "Spread of Black Consciousness," in *Black Review 1972,* ed. Bennie Khoapa (Durban: Black Community Programmes, 1973), p. 45.

3.   Barney Pityana, "Power and Social Change in South Africa," in *Student Perspectives on South Africa,* ed. Hendrik W. Van der Merwe and David Welsh (Cape Town: David Philip Publisher, 1972), p. 185. Hereafter cited as: Pityana, *Power.*

4.   Biko, *I Write What I Like,* ed. Alfred Stubbs (New York: Harper and Row, 1978), p. 23. Hereafter cited as: Biko, *I Write.* The full quotation is taken as cited in James Cone, *Black Theology and Black Power* (New York: The Seabury Press, 1969), p. 24. Hereafter cited as: Cone, *Black Theology.*

5.   Ranwedzi Nengwekhulu, *The Meaning of Black Consciousness in the Struggle for Liberation in South Africa* (United Nations, No. 16/76, July 1976), p. 2. Hereafter cited as: Nengwekhulu, *The Meaning of Black Consciousness.*

6.   Biko, *I Write,* pp. 21–22.

7.   Bennie A. Khoapa, "The New Black," in *Black Viewpoint,* ed. Steve Biko (Durban: SPRO-CAS, 1972), p. 66. Hereafter cited as: Khoapa, *The New Black.*

8.   Biko, *I Write,* p. 24.

9.   Bonganjalo Goba, "Corporate Personality: Ancient Israel and Africa," in *The Challenge of Black Theology in South Africa,* ed. Basil Moore (Atlanta: John Knox Press, 1974), p. 69.

10.   *Ibid.*

11.   Manas Buthelezi, "An African Theology or a Black Theology?" in *The Challenge of Black Theology in South Africa,* ed. Basil Moore (Atlanta: John Knox Press, 1974), p. 34. Hereafter cited as: Buthelezi, *An African Theology.*

12.   S. T. M. Magagula, "Black Power," (Unpublished paper, 1973).

13.   Khoapa, *The New Black,* p. 64.

14.   Njabulo Ndebele, "Black Development," in *Black Viewpoint,* ed. Steve Biko (Durban: SPRO-CAS, 1972), p. 14. Hereafter cited as: Ndebele, *Black Development.*

15.   Foszia Fisher and Harold Nxasana, "The Labour Situation in South Africa," *South African Labour Bulletin,* 2, 2 (July 1975), p. 45. Reproduced under the same title in *Black Renaissance, Papers from the Black Renaissance Convention,* ed. Thoahlane Thoahlane (Johannesburg: Ravan Press, 1975), pp. 53–58.

16.   *Ibid.,* p. 45.

17.   *Ibid.,* pp. 45–46.

18.   *Ibid.,* p. 50.

19.   *Ibid.,* pp. 46–47.

20.   Ndebele, *Black Development,* p. 22.

21.   Eugene D. Genovese, *Roll, Jordan, Roll* (New York: Vintage Books, 1976), pp. 385–386. Hereafter cited as: Genovese, *Roll.*

22.   "The Transkei Independence," *SASO Newsletter,* 6, 1 (March/April 1976), p. 2. Hereafter cited as: SASO, *The Transkei.*

23.   *Ibid.*

24.   Z. Mothopeng, "Imperialist Penetration into African Universities," *SASO Newsletter,* 5, a (July/August 1975), pp. 4–5.

25.   "Apartheid and the Anti-Imperialist Struggle," *SASO Newsletter,* 5, 3 (November/December 1975), p. 5. Hereafter cited as: SASO, *Apartheid.*

26.   *Ibid.*

27. Ndebele, *Black Development*, pp. 16–17.

28. *Ibid.*

29. *Ibid.*

30. *Ibid.*, p. 23.

31. This is why SASO set up in 1972 the "Black Workers Project" whose objectives were

> to act as a co-ordinating body to serve the needs and aspirations of black workers; to unite and bring about solidarity of black workers; to conscientise them about their role and obligation toward black development; to run clinics for leadership, in-service training and imbue them with pride and self-confidence as people and about their potential as workers. (Quoted as cited in *Black Review 1972*, ed. Bennie Khoapa, Durban: Black Community Programmes, 1973), p. 27.

32. Paulo Freire, *Pedagogy of the Oppressed*, trans. Myra Bergman Ramos (New York: The Seabury Press, 1974), p. 169. Hereafter cited as: Freire, *Pedagogy*. There is evidence that Paulo Freire's conceptions on education as the development of a critical consciousness had a strong impact on Black Consciousness. See Steve Biko, *Black Consciousness in South Africa,* ed. Arnold Millard (New York: Vintage Books, 1979), p. 285. Hereafter cited as: Biko, *Black Consciousness.* Although Biko incorrectly used the name Paul Lafrere for Paulo Freire, there is no doubt that he was speaking of Freire.

33. Paulo Freire, *Education for Critical Consciousness*, trans. Center for the Study of Development and Social Change (New York: The Seabury Press, 1973), pp. 5–6.

34. Mafika Gwala, "Black Community Programmes," in *Black Review 1973,* ed. Mafika Gwala (Durban: Black Community Programmes, 1974), p. 165.

35. Nkosazana Dlamini, "Soweto Student Speaks Out, Interview with Nknosazana Dlamini, Vice President of SASO," *Southern Africa,* X, 2 (March 1977), p. 7.

36. Nengwekhulu, *The Meaning of Black Consciousness*, pp. 4–5.

37. *Ibid.*, p. 5.

38. D. A. Kotze, *African Politics in South Africa, 1964–1974* (New York: St. Martin's Press, 1975), p. 89. Hereafter cited as: Kotze, *African Politics.*

39. See Bennie Khoapa, "Youth and Student Organizations," in *Black Review 1972,* ed. Bennie Khoapa (Durban: Black Community Programmes, 1973), pp. 181–184. Hereafter cited as: Khoapa, *Youth.* See also Makika Gwala, "Youth and Student Organizations," in *Black Review 1973,* ed. Mafika Gwala (Durban: Black Community Programmes, 1974), pp. 62–66.

40. Alan Brooks and Jeremy Brickhill, *Whirlwind Before the Storm* (London: International Defence and Aid Fund for Southern Africa, 1980), pp. 85–98. Hereafter cited as: Brooks and Brickhill, *Whirlwind.*

41. *Ibid.*, p. 89.

42. Khoapa, *Youth,* p. 182.

43. Brooks and Brickhill, *Whirlwind,* p. 88.

44. *Ibid.*, pp. 89–126.

45. Ranwedzi Nengwekhulu, "Black Consciousness Movement of South Africa," Speech given to the Assembly of the IUEF held in Geneva (November 22, 1976), p. 3.

46. Brooks and Brickhill, *Whirlwind,* p. 74.

47. Cited in Biko, *Black Consciousness,* p. 162.

48.   Brooks and Brickhill, *Whirlwind,* p. 76.

49.   "Black Communalism," *Pro Veritate* (June 1976), pp. 6–7. Hereafter cited as: Communalism, *Pro Veritate.*

50.   Tami Zani, "The Future Society as seen by Black People's Convention," *Pro Veritate* (June 1977), p. 11. Hereafter cited as: Zani, *The Future.*

51.   Denis Goulet, *The Cruel Choice* (New York; Atheneum, 1975), p. 256.

52.   Communalism, *Pro Veritate,* p. 7.

53.   *Ibid.*

54.   Zani, *The Future,* p. 11.

55.   For Nyerere's influence see Pityana, *Power,* pp. 180–181. For Cabral's and Machel's influence see SASO, *Apartheid.* For Kaunda's influence see Biko, *I Write,* p. 46.

56.   Biko, *I Write,* pp. 46–47.

Chapter V

1.   Basil Moore, Preface," in *The Challenge of Black Theology in South Africa,* ed. Basil Moore (Atlanta: John Knox, 1974), p. IX. Hereafter cited as: Moore, *Preface.*

2.   Sabelo Ntwasa, "The Concept of The Church in Black Theology," in *The Challenge of Black Theology in South Africa,* ed. Basil Moore (Atlanta: John Knox, 1974), p. 112. Hereafter cited as: Ntwasa, *The Church.*

3.   Friedrich Nietzsche, *Beyond Good and Evil,* translated with introduction by Marianne Gowan (Chicago: Gateway Editions, 1955), p. 55.

4.   Moore, *Preface,* p. VIII.

5.   James Cone, *Black Theology and Black Power* (New York: The Seabury Press, 1969), p. 38.

6.   Allan Boesak, *Farewell to Innocence* (Johannesburg: Ravan Press, 1976), pp. 112–113. Hereafter cited as: Boesak, *Farewell.*

7.   Basil Moore, "What is Black Theology?" in *The Challenge of Black Theology in South Africa,* ed. Basil Moore (Atlanta: John Knox, 1974), p. 8. Hereafter cited as: Moore, *What is Black Theology?*

8.   James Cone, "Black Theology and Black Liberation," in *The Challenge of Black Theology in South Africa,* ed. Basil Moore (Atlanta: John Knox, 1974), p. 53.

9.   Robert Birt, "An Examination of James Cone's Concept of God and Its Role in Black Liberation," *The Philosophical Forum,* IX, 2–3 (Winter/Spring 1977–1978), p. 346.

10.   Gustavo Gutierrez, *A Theology of Liberation,* trans. Sister Caridad Inda and John Eagleson (New York: Orbis Books, 1973), p. 177. Hereafter cited as: Gutierrez, *Liberation.*

11.   Sabelo Ntwasa and Basil Moore, "The Concept of God in Black Theology," in *The Challenge of Black Theology in South Africa,* ed. Basil Moore (Atlanta: John Knox, 1974), pp. 24–26.

12.   Manas Buthelezi, "An African Theology or a Black Theology?" in *The Challenge of Black Theology in South Africa,* ed. Basil Moore (Atlanta: John Knox Press, 1974), pp. 32, 33.

13.   *Ibid.,* p. 33.

14. David Bosch, "Currents and Crosscurrents in South African Black Theology," *Journal of Religion in Africa,* VI, (1974), p. 8.
15. Ntwasa, *The Church,* p. 117.
16. Mokgethi Motlhabi, "Black Theology and Authority," in *The Challenge of Black Theology in South Africa,* ed. Basil Moore (Atlanta: John Knox, 1974), p. 127. Hereafter cited as: Motlhabi, *Black Theology.*
17. Biko, *I Write,* p. 93.
18. As cited in Gutierrez, *Liberation,* p. 7.
19. Mokgethi Motlhabi, "Black Theology: A Personal View," in *The Challenge of Black Theology in South Africa,* ed. Basil Moore (Atlanta: John Knox, 1974), pp. 74–75.
20. John W. de Gruchy, *The Church Struggle in South Africa* (Grand Rapids: William B. Eerdmans Publishing Company, 1979), p. 182. Hereafter cited as: de Gruchy, *The Church.*
21. Boesak, *Farewell,* pp. 116–117.
22. Moore, *What is Black Theology?,* pp. 3–4.
23. Archie Mafeje, "Religion, Class and Ideology in South Africa," in *Religion and Social Change in Southern Africa,* ed. Michel G. Whisson and Martin West (Cape Town: 1975), p. 177.
24. Genovese, *Roll,* pp. 659–660.
25. Manas Buthelezi, "Black Christians Must Liberate Whites," *Reality,* 5, 3 (July 1973), p. 6.
26. As quoted in de Gruchy, *The Church,* p. 186.
27. Max Weber, *From Max Weber,* ed. H. H. Gerth and C. Wright Mills (New York: Oxford University Press, 1958), p. 121.
28. Boesak, *Farewell,* p. 58.
29. Freire, *Pedagogy,* p. 42.
30. Boesak, *Farewell,* p. 58.
31. E. J. Hobsbawm, *Primitive Rebels* (New York: Norton Library, 1959), p. 60.

Chapter VI

1. The other organizations banned were ASSECA, the Black Parents Association, the Black Women's Federation, the Border Youth Organization, the Christian Institute of Southern Africa, the Eastern Province Youth Organization, the Medupe Writers' Association, the Natal Youth Organization, the National Youth Organization, the South African Students' Movement (SASM), the Soweto Students Representative Council, the Transvaal Youth Organization, the Union of Black Journalists, the Western Cape Youth Organization, the Zimele Trust and the Black Community Programmes.
2. Department of Defence, Republic of South Africa, *White Paper on Defence, 1977,* as quoted in Richard Leonard, *South Africa at War* (Westport: Lawrence Hill & Company, 1983), p. 200.
3. The formation in October 1979 of the Azanian People's Organization (AZAPO) testifies to the vitality and growing radicalization of the Black Consciousness Move-

ment. Determined to mobilize the workers for their liberation and to stress the primacy of economic structures in the struggle for a new order, AZAPO appears to confirm the validity of our thesis on the revolutionary character of Black Consciousness. See *The Star, International Airmail Weekly* (Johannesburg), October 6, p. 7. See also *Survey of Race Relations*, 1979, pp. 50–51, in which the declared objectives of AZAPO are defined as follows:

> (1) to conscientise, politicise and mobilise black workers through the philosophy of black consciousness [and] to strive for their legitimate rights; (2) to work towards the establishment of an educational system that would respond creatively towards the needs of Azanians; (3) to promote an interpretation of religion as a liberatory philosophy relevant to the black struggle; (4) to promote and encourage research into various problems affecting the people; (5) to expose the oppressive exploitative system in which black people are denied basic human rights; and (6) to work towards the unity of the oppressed for the just distribution of wealth and power to all people of Azania.

4.   See Heribert Adam, "The Rise of Black Consciousness in South Africa," *Race*, XV, 2 (October 1973), pp. 149–165. Kotze, *African Politics*, pp. 97–98. René Lefort, *L'Afrique du Sud: Histoire d'une Crise* (Paris: Maspéro, 1977), pp. 121–123. Hereafter cited as: Lefort, *Crise*. "Black Consciousness—Ten Years After," *Student Representative Council, University of Cape Town* (1978).

5.   D. A. Kotze, *African Politics in South Africa, 1964-1974* (New York: St. Martin's Press, 1975), p. 98. See also Archie Mafeje, "Soweto and its Aftermath," in *South African Capitalism and Black Political Opposition*, ed. Martin J. Murray (Cambridge: Schenkman Publishing Company, 1982), pp. 739–759; Mafeje contends that:

> It is not unfair to state that the ideology of 'Black Consciousness' remains vacuous in the South African circumstances. Not only does it eschew the question of imperialism in general and of capitalist exploitation inside and around South Africa, but it can also hardly be considered a historical advance on the older nationalist movement such as PAC. . . . (p. 749).

6.   Lefort, *Crise*, p. 121.

7.   See Baruch Hirson, *Year of Fire, Year of Ash. The Soweto Revolt: Roots of a Revolution?* (London: Zed Press, 1979), pp. 127–130. Hereafter cited as: Hirson, *Year of Fire.*

8.   *Ibid.,* p. 130.

9.   Alan Brooks and Jeremy Brickhill, *Whirlwind Before the Storm* (London: International Defence and Aid Fund for Southern Africa, 1980), pp. 215–225. Hereafter cited as: Brooks and Brickhill, *Whirlwind.*

10.   Hirson, *Year of Fire*, p. 143.

11.   Brooks and Brickhill, *Whirlwind*, pp. 151–152.

12.   *Ibid.,* pp. 198–238.

13.   *Ibid.,* p. 228.

14.   Tom Lodge, *Black Politics in South Africa Since 1945*, (New York: Longman, 1983), pp. 330–356. Hereafter cited as: Lodge, *Black Politics.*

15.   Raymond Franklin, "The Political Economy of Black Power," *Social Problems*, 16, 3 (Winter 1969), p. 294.

16.   Leo Marquard, "Black Consciousness," *Reality*, 5, 4 (September 1973), p. 10. Herafter cited as: Marquard, *Black.*

17. *Ibid.*, p. 10. See also Philip Frankel, "Black Power in South Africa," *New Nation*, 6, 3 (October 1972), p. 3. What the *East London Daily Dispatch* wrote about SASO's emergence is a good example of the liberals' views: "The promoters of SASO are wrong in what they are doing. They are promoting apartheid. They are entrenching the idea of racial exclusivity and therefore doing the Government's work." Cited as quoted in Gerhart, *Black Power in South Africa* (Berkeley: University of California Press, 1978), pp. 45–84. Hereafter cited as: Gerhart, *Black Power.*

18. Steve Biko, *I Write What I Like,* edited by Alfred Stubbs (New York: Harper & Row, 1978), p. 91.

19. Gerhart, *Black Power,* pp. 45–84. Peter Walshe, *Black Nationalism in South Africa* (Johannesburg: Ravan Press, 1973), pp. 26–35.

20. "Apartheid and the Anti-Imperialist Struggle," *SASO Newsletter,* 5, 3 (November/December 1975), p. 4.

21. As quoted in "Steve Biko: Organizer for Freedom," *Southern Africa,* X, 8 (October 1977), p. 10.

22. The roots and importance of the Soweto uprisings remain a subject of considerable debate. For my purposes, a general study of these uprisings is unnecessary. However, a considerable amount of literature has already been devoted to this period of black resistance. The three most important books are: Hirson, *Year of Fire;* Brickhill and Brooks, *Whirlwind;* John Kane-Berman, *South Africa: The Method in the Madness* (London: Pluto Press,, 1978). Hereafter cited as: Kane-Berman, *South Africa.* For an excellent review of the literature on Soweto see Frank Molteno, "The Uprising of 16th June: A Review of the Literature on Events in South Africa 1976," *Social Dynamics,* 5, 1 (1979), pp. 54–89. Another article of interest is: Archie Mafeje, "Soweto and its Aftermath," *Review of African Political Economy,* 11 (January–April 1978), pp. 17–30. Finally see: Lodge, *Black Politics,* pp. 321–362.

23. Antonio Gramsci, *Selections from Prison Notebooks,* ed. and trans. by Quintin Hoare and Geoffrey Nowell Smith (London: Lawrence and Wishart, 1973), pp. 229–245. Hereafter cited as: Gramsci, *Notebooks.* As Anne Showstack Sassoon describes it, the "war of position"

> involves wide-ranging social organization and cultural influence, and it is only victory on these fronts which makes possible or conclusive a frontal attack or war of movement. Gramsci says that a war of position continues after the transformation of state power and while a new society is built and consolidated. (Anne Showstack Sassoon ed., *Approaches to Gramsci,* London: Writers and Readers, 1982), p. 17. Hereafter cited as: Sassoon, *Gramsci.*)

24. See Gramsci, *Notebooks,* pp. 229–245. The "war of movement" is the revolutionary moment and it indicates the violence of the confrontation between antagonistic classes for the seizure of state power. The "war of movement" is symbolized by the Bolschevik Revolution of 1917 and it is more likely to occur where civil society has failed to develop to full maturity. Finally, it can be said that for Gramsci the "war of movement" was the culmination of the travail of the "war of position." See Sassoon, *Gramsci,* p. 16.

25. Kane-Berman, *South Africa,* pp. 217–229.

26. "Our Urgent Task," *Solidarity,* No. 4 (October 1980), p. 8.

27. Saths Cooper, "Main Address," *Azanian People's Organization,* February 1983, p. 16. Hereafter cited as: Cooper, *Address.*

28. The constitutional proposals made by the ruling National Party and adopted by the white electorate in November 1983 are an attempt to integrate "Coloured" and Asians as junior partners in the white power structure. These proposals entail neither the end of white supremacy nor the incorporation of Africans into the political system. At best, they are a means of coopting some sectors of the Asian and "Coloured" petty bourgeoisies into the defense of apartheid. The details of the new constitution as described by the pro-governmental *Southern African Facts Sheet,* 40 (October 1982), pp. 2–3, are as follows:

> The National Party's constitutional plan is based on the twin pillars of self-determination for each of the three groups (Whites, Coloureds and Asians) in respect of their own affairs and joint responsibility of all three groups on matters of common interest. Towards this end, a constitutional structure has been proposed that has four main components: Parliament, the President, the Executive and the President's Council.
>
> There will be a single Parliament for Whites, Coloureds and Asians. This joint institution will be tricameral with separate chambers from the three population groups. Each of these population groups will elect its own chamber on its own voters roll [the White chamber will be the present House of Assembly]. Each chamber will decide exclusively on matters affecting the affairs of its own group.
>
> Matters of common concern for the White, Coloured and Asian communities will be decided by the three chambers, sitting separately, by simple majority vote. The principle of consensus will be fundamental to this new structure and agreement among the three chambers will be promoted by referring legislation on common affairs to joint committees. In the event of disagreement leading to a deadlock, however, the President's Council will act as the final arbiter. Its role in this regard will be purely one of arbitration and it will not be able to initiate legislation.
>
> The President will be an executive head of state and will combine the present two offices of State President and Prime Minister. He may not be a Member of Parliament while serving as head of state but may remain the leader of his party. He will be elected by an electoral college consisting of 50 White, 25 Coloured and 13 Asian members [this being the rough ratio of their numerical strength in the population composition as a whole]. The members of the electoral college will be appointed by their respective chambers, the practical effect of this being that the ruling party in each chamber will contribute all the members of the electoral college from its particular chamber.
>
> The President will decide which matters are separate issues to be submitted to a particular chamber of Parliament and which matters are common issues to be decided upon by all three chambers. He will appoint and preside over the Cabinet.
>
> The Cabinet will be a joint institution to which a fixed number of Ministers will be appointed. Ministers will be chosen on merit from the White, Coloured and Asian communities and there will be no fixed proportional representation. Not all Ministers need be Members of Parliament. Cabinet committees consisting of Ministers of the respective population groups will deal with those affairs and legislation pertaining to their particular group.

Once again, the principle of consensus will be fundamental to the functioning of the Cabinet.

The President's Council will consist of 60 members. The respective chambers of Parliament will elect 20 whites, 10 Coloured and 5 Asian members to the Council and the remaining 25 members will be nominated by the President.

In addition to being the final arbiter in the event of disputes in Parliament, the President's Council will advise the President at his request on matters of national interest.

At the local government level the NP proposals provide for White, Coloured and Asian communities to have their own local authorities such as town councils that will enjoy the greatest possible degree of local autonomy and will decide their own affairs themselves. Such local authorities might then be grouped in metropolitan and/or regional councils that will undertake common services such as water supply. Changes in the second tier of government, the provincial system, are also envisaged in due course.

29. Stuart Hall, "Moving Right," *Socialist Review*, 55 (1981), pp. 113–137. Hereafter cited as: Hall, *Right*.

30. John Saul and Stephen Gelb, *The Crisis in South Africa* (New York: Monthly Review Press, 1981), pp. 45–90. Hereafter cited as: Saul and Gelb, *The Crisis*.

31. Sassoon, *Gramsci*, p. 133.

32. Gramsci, *Notebooks*, p. 181.

33. Sassoon, *Gramsci*, p. 15.

34. Gramsci, *Notebooks*, p. 178.

35. *Ibid.*, p. 177.

36. Hall, *Right*, p. 117.

37. *Ibid.*

38. *Ibid.*

39. Sam C. Nolutshungu, *Changing South Africa. Political Considerations*, (Manchester: Manchester University Press, 1982), p. 106.

40. *The Guardian*, September 21, 1983, p. 14; see also *Tokoloho*, Vol. 1, no. 1, p. 3; *Solidarity News Service*, No. 3, 83, p. 4.

41. *Solidarity News Service*, no. 3, 83, p. 4.

42. *The Guardian*, September 21, 1983, p. 14.

43. See: Baruch Hirson, *Year of Fire*, p. 328. See also Richard Leonard, *South Africa at War* (Westport: Lawrence Hill & Company, 1983), pp. 21–58.

44. Kane-Berman, *South Africa*, p. 217.

45. "ANC President Explains the Struggle," *Sechaba*, 11 (Fourth Quarter 1977), p. 11. A similar view is expressed in R. S. Nyameko and G. Singh, "The Role of Black Consciousness in the South African Revolution," *The African Communist*, 68 (First Quarter 1977), pp. 34–47.

46. I have introduced the term "national Africanist" to express the Africanist origins and beliefs of a rather conservative and chauvinistic wing of black nationalism in South Africa.

The eight "national Africanists" to whom I will allude subsequently are: T. Bonga, A. M. Makiwane, J. D. Matlow, G. M. Mbele, A. K. Mquota, P. Ngakane, T. X. Makiwane and O. K. Setlhapelo. Their explanation for their breakaway from the ANC is to be found in the following documents: "Statement on the Expulsion from the ANC of South Africa," *Ikwezi*, II, 1 (March 1975), pp. 29–36. Hereafter cited as: Ikwezi, *Expulsion,* And in the pamphlet African National Congress of South Africa (African Nationalists), *In Defence of the African Image and Heritage* (Dar Es Salaam: February 1976). Hereafter cited as: African Nationalists, *African Image.* What precipitated the expulsion of these eight National Africanists was a speech made by Alfred Kogkong Mquota at the funeral of Robert Resha who was a member of the National Executive of the ANC. At this same funeral Mzimkulu Ambrose Makiwane made a similar speech which had a similar impact. These two speeches are reproduced as an Appendix in *Ikwezi,* 1, 1 (November 1975), pp. 21–24. Both speeches condemned the "multiracialism" of the ANC which led, so it was argued, to its "hi-jack" by "White petty-bourgeois communists." They demanded the "re-Africanisation" of the ANC and consequently a return to the old policy of exclusive African membership.

Ikwezi is a periodical which carries a virulent assault on the ANC and the South African Communist Party. In its first issue published in November 1975 it defined itself as a "Marxist-Leninist" journal. It attacked the South African Communist Party because it considered it a "revisionist" force which was "totally bankrupt and corrupt" and which was "nothing more that the agent of Soviet social-imperialism." Since the ANC was, according to Ikwezi, the tool of the "white petty-bourgeois intellectuals" of the Communist Party, it represented an even more "bankrupt and corrupt" movement.

Despite its revolutionary rhetoric and its Maoist phraseology, Ikwezi was more a journal of African nationalism than of a truly Marxist-Leninist movement. It was committed to "Africanism" and to the rejection of "multiracialism." It stood closer to the PAC than any other South African movement of liberation. See "Editorial— P. K. Leballo Expelled: But can the PAC Revive Itself from the Ashes of 'Leballoism'," *Ikwezi,* 13 (October 1979), pp. 1–2.

The justification for the expulsion from the ANC was provided in two documents. The first was the official statement of the ANC which was published as "Conspirators Expelled," *Sechaba,* 10, 2 (Second Quarter 1976), pp. 40–43. The second was a more elaborate discussion of what was described as the "Ghetto nationalism of the petty-bourgeoisie." This document came from the central committee of the South African Communist Party and was published as: "The Enemy Hidden Under the Same Colour," *The African Communist,* 65 (Second Quarter 1976), pp. 16–40.

48.   Ikwezi, *Expulsion,* p. 31.

49.   African Nationalists, *African Image,* p. 6.

50.   Alfred Nzo, *Interviews in Depth, South Africa, African National Congress* (Richmond: LSM Press, 1974), p. 15.

51.   "Inside South Africa: A New Movement is Formed," *Sechaba,* 7, 3 (March 1973), p. 5.

52.   "Forward to the Armed Seizure of Power," in *ANC Speaks: Documents and Statements of the African National Congress,* 1955–1976, published by the ANC (September 1977), pp. 140–141. Hereafter cited as: ANC, *Seizure of Power.*

53.   *Ibid.,* p. 141.

54.   The term "middle-class solution" is borrowed from Basil Davidson and it expresses the attempts of African leaders, in the post-colonial era, to build their own capitalist systems of production on the basis of the inherited economic and political structures of the imperialist era. These attempts have either failed or contributed to what has been called "growth without development." See Basil Davidson, *Can Africa Survive? Arguments Against Growth Without Development.* (Boston: Atlantic—Little, Brown Books, 1974).

55. The ambiguity of the policies to be adopted towards the Bantustans is revealed in the different views that were held inside the Central Committee of the South African Communist Party. See, "Bantustans; Black Consciousness; White opposition," *The African Communist,* 57 (Second Quarter 1974), pp. 25–33.

56. Inkatha's aims are certainly not nationalist, let alone revolutionary. Their power base rests on the Zulu ethnic group and on the relative popularity of Chief Gatsha Buthelezi. Although lip service has been paid to the concept of a unitary South Africa, the main idea behind Inkatha is to "foster the spirit of unity among the people of the Zulu nation throughout South Africa, and to keep alive and foster the Zulu Nation's traditions and a sense among the Nation of the obligations . . . towards the other races of . . . South Africa." Quoted as cited in Lawrence Schlemmer and Tim J. Muil, "Social and Political Change in the African Areas: A Case Study of Kwazulu," in *Change in Contemporary South Africa,* ed. Leonard Thompson and Jeffery Butler (Berkeley: University of California Press, 1975), p. 123.

It is no wonder that the prospects of an alliance, even a tactical one, between the ANC and Inkatha must be worrisome for anyone concerned about the radical transformation of South Africa from its current racist and class structures.

57. Oliver Tambo, "Unity in Action—Decisive," *New African,* 151 (March 1980), p. 60.

58. Joe Slovo, "South Africa—No Middle Road," in *Southern Africa: The New Politics of Revolution,* ed. Basil Davidson, Joe Slovo and Anthony R. Wilkinson (Harmondsworth: Penguin Books, 1976), pp. 195–196.

59. Tebello Motapanyane, "How June 16 Demo was Planned," *Sechaba,* 11 (Second Quarter 1977), pp. 53–54.

60. Tsietsi Mashinini quoted as cited in Kane-Berman, *South Africa,* p. 145.

61. Tsietsi Mashinini quoted as cited in Hirson, *Year of Fire,* p. 245.

62. The growing importance of the revolutionary underground is well documented in Kane-Berman, *South Africa,* pp. 144–146 and 217–229. See also Hirson, *Year of Fire,* pp. 199–201, p. 245, pp. 251–252, and pp. 327–328. See finally Alexander Sibeko, "The Underground Voice," *The African Communist,* 68 (First Quarter 1977), pp. 48–58.

63. Mosima Sexwale quoted as cited in Kane-Berman, *South Africa,* pp. 223–224.

64. ANC, *Seizure of Power,* p. 141.

65. Andrew Shonfield, *Modern Capitalism. The Changing Balance of Public and Private Power* (Oxford: Oxford University Press, 1965); John Kenneth Galbraith, *The New Industrial State* (New York, New America Library, 1971); for a comprehensive Marxist critique of the "welfare state" see Ernest Mandel, *Late Capitalism* (London: Verso Edition, 1978).

66. International Defence & Aid Fund, *The Apartheid War Machine* (London: IDAF, 1980), pp. 3–4.

67. The extent of state violence in South Africa is well documented. See for example: Allen Cook, *South Africa: The Imprisoned Society* (International Defense and Aid Fund: 1974); A. Sachs, *The Violence of Apartheid* (London: International Defense and Aid Fund, 1970).

68. Amilcar Cabral, *Unity and Struggle. Speeches and Writings of Amilcar Cabral* (New York: Monthly Review Press, 1979), p. 123.

BIBLIOGRAPHY

Books

Adam, Heribert (ed.). *South Africa: Sociological Perspectives.* New York: Oxford University Press, 1971.
———. *Modernizing Racial Domination.* Berkeley: University of California Press, 1971.
———, and Giliomee, Hermann. *Ethnic Power Mobilized.* New Haven: Yale University Press, 1979.
Adamson, Walter L. *Hegemony and Revolution.* Berkeley: University of California Press, 1980.
Benson, Mary. *South Africa: The Struggle for a Birthright.* Minerva Press, 1969.
Biko, Steve. *I Write What I Like.* Edited by Alfred Stubbs. New York: Harper & Row, 1978.
———. *Black Consciousness in South Africa.* Edited and introduced by Arnold Millard. New York: Vintage Books, 1979.
Boesak, Allan. *Farewell to Innocence.* Johannesburg: Ravan Press, 1976.
Boggs, Carl. *Gramsci's Marxism.* London: Pluto Press, 1976.
Brooks, Alan and Brickhill, Jeremy. *Whirlwind Before The Storm.* London: International Defence and Aid Fund for Southern Africa, 1980.
Brotz, Howard. *The Politics of S. A.* Oxford: Oxford University Press, 1977.
Cabral, Amilcar. *Unity and Struggle.* Introduced by Basil Davidson. New York: Monthly Review Press, 1979.
Callinicos, Alex, and Rogers, John. *Southern Africa After Soweto.* London: Pluto Press, 1978.
Carmichael, Stokley, and Hamilton, Charles. *Black Power.* New York: Random House, 1967.

Cleaver, Eldridge. *Soul on Ice*. New York: McGraw Hill, 1967.

Cohn, Norman. *The Pursuit of the Millenium*. 2nd ed. revised. New York: Harper & Row, 1961.

Cone, James. *Black Theology and Black Power*. New York: The Seabury Press, 1969.

Cox, Oliver C. *Caste, Class, and Race*. New York: Monthly Review Press, 1970.

Davidson, Basil. *Can Africa Survive?* Boston: An Atlantic Monthly Press Book, Little, Brown and Company, 1974.

———, Slovo, Joe, and Wilkinson, Anthony (ed.). *Southern Africa: The New Politics of Revolution*. Harmondsworth: Penguin Books, 1976.

———. *Let Freedom Come: Africa in Modern History*. Boston: An Atlantic Monthly Press Book, 1978.

Davies, Robert H. *Class, State and White Labour in South Africa: 1900–1960*. Atlantic Highlands: Humanities Press, 1979.

Davis, Horace B. *Toward a Marxist Theory of Nationalism*. New York: Monthly Review Press, 1978.

De Gruchy, John. *The Church Struggle in South Africa*. Grand Rapids: Eerdmans Publishing Company, 1979.

De Kiewiet, C. W. *A History of South Africa*. New York: Oxford University Press, 1957.

Emmerson, Donald K. (ed.). *Students and Politics in Developing Nations*. New York: Frederick A. Praeger, 1968.

Fanon, Frantz. *Wretched of the Earth*. New York: Grove Press, Inc., 1967.

———. *Black Skin, White Masks*. New York: Grove Press, Inc., 1967.

Fiori, Guiseppe. *Antonio Gramsci: Life of a Revolutionary*. London: New Left Books, 1970.

Foreign Policy Study Foundation. *South Africa: Time Running Out. The Report of the Study Commission on U.S. Policy Toward Southern Africa*. Berkeley: University of California Press, 1981.

Franklin, Raymond S., and Resnik, Solomon. *The Political Economy of Racism*. Hinsdale, Illinois: Dryden Press, 1973.

Freire, Paulo. *Education for Critical Consciousness*. New York: The Seabury Press, 1973.

Freire, Paulo. *Pedagogy of the Oppressed*. New York: The Seabury Press, 1974.

Genovese, Eugene D. *The Political Economy of Slavery*. New York: Vintage Books Edition, 1967.

————. *The World the Slaveholders Made*. New York: Vintage Books Edition, 1971.

————. *The Red and Black: Marxian Explorations in Southern and Afro-American History*. New York: Pantheon Books, 1971.

————. *Roll, Jordan, Roll*. New York: Vintage Books Edition, 1976.

Gerhart, Gail. *Black Power in South Africa*. Berkeley: University of California Press, 1978.

Gordon, Loraine; Blignaut, Suzanne; Moroney, Sean; and Cooper, Carole (ed.). *A Survey of Race Relations in South Africa, 1977*. Johannesburg: South African Institute of Race Relations, 1978.

Goulet, Denis. *The Cruel Choice*. New York: Atheneum, 1975.

Gramsci, Antonio. *Selections From the Prison Notebooks of Antonio Gramsci*. Translated and edited by Quintin Hoare and Geoffrey Nowell Smith. London: Lawrence and Wishart, 1971.

Gutierrez, Gustavo. *A Theology of Liberation*. Maryknoll, New York: Orbis Boods, 1973.

Hirson, Baruch. *Year of Fire, Year of Ash*. London: Zed Press, 1979.

Hobsbawn, Eric. *Primitive Rebels*. New York: Norton and Company, 1959.

Hodgkin, Thomas. *Nationalism in Colonial Africa*. New York: New York University Press, 1957.

Honderich, Ted. *Violence For Equality*. Harmondsworth: Penguin Books, 1980.

Horrell, Muriel (ed.). *A Survey of Race Relations in South Africa, 1969*. Johannesburg: South African Institute of Race Relations, 1970.

————. *A Survey of Race Relations in South Africa, 1970*. Johannesburg: South African Institute of Race Relations, 1971.

Horrell, Muriel; Horner, Dudley; and Kane-Berman, John (ed.). *A Survey of Race Relations in South Africa, 1971*. Johannesburg: South African Institute of Race Relations, 1972.

Horrell, Muriel; Horner, Dudley; Kane-Berman, John; and Margo, Robin (ed.). *A Survey of Race Relations in South Africa, 1972*. Johannesburg: South African Institute of Race Relations, 1973.

Horrell, Muriel; Horner, Dudley (ed.). *A Survey of Race Relations in South Africa, 1973*. Johannesburg: South African Institute of Race Relations, 1974.

————; ————; and Hudson, Jane (ed.). *A Survey of Race Relations in South Africa, 1974*. Johannesburg: South African Institute of Race Relations, 1976.

————; ————; Blignaut, Suzanne; Moroney, Sean (ed.). *A Survey of Race Relations in South Africa, 1976.* Johannesburg: South African Institute of Race Relations, 1977.

Horwitz, Ralph. *The Political Economy of South Africa.* New York: Frederick A. Praeger, 1967.

International Defence and Aid Fund. *The Apartheid War Machine.* London: IDAF, 1980.

Kane-Berman, John. *South Africa: The Method in the Madness.* London: Pluto Press, 1978.

Karis, Thomas, and Carter, Gwendolen M. (ed.). *From Protest to Challenge.* Volume 2. Stanford: Stanford University, 1977.

————; ————; and Gerhart, Gail (ed.). *From Protest to Challenge. Volume 3.* Stanford: Stanford University, 1977.

Kedourie, Elie. *Nationalism.* London: Hutchinson University Library, 1966.

Khoapa, Bennie (ed.). *Black Review 1972.* Durban: Black Community Programmes, 1973.

Klerk, de W. A. *The Puritans in Africa: A History of Afrikanerdom.* Harmondsworth: Penguin Books, 1976.

Kohn, Hans. *Nationalism: Its Meaning and History.* New York: D. Van Nostrand Company, Inc., 1955.

Kotze, D. A. *African Politics in South Africa, 1964–1974.* New York: St. Martin's Press, 1975.

Kuper, Leo. *Passive Resistance in South Africa.* New Haven: Yale University Press, 1957.

————. *An African Bourgeoisie, Race, Class and Politics in South Africa.* New Haven: Yale University Press, 1965.

Kuper, Leo. *Race, Class and Power.* London: Dukworth, 1974.

La Guma, Alex (ed.). *Apartheid.* New York: International Publishers, 1971.

Lefort, René. *L'Afrique du Sud: Histoire d'une Crise.* Paris: Maspéro, 1977.

Legassick, Martin. *The National Union of South African Students: Ethnic Cleavage and Ethnic Integration in the Universities.* Los Angeles: African Studies Center, University of California, Occasional Paper Number 4, 1967.

Leonard, Richard. *South Africa at War.* Westport: Lawrence Hill & Company, 1983.

Lewin, Julius. *Politics and Law in South Africa.* London: Merlin Press, 1963.

Lodge, Tom. *Black Politics in South Africa Since 1945.* New York: Longman, 1983.

Lutuli, Albert. *Let My People Go: An Autobiography.* London: Collins, 1962.

Magubane, Bernard M. *The Political Economy of Race and Class in South Africa.* New York: Monthly Review Press, 1979.

Malcolm X. *The Autobiography of Malcolm X.* Edited by Alex Haley. New York: Grove Press, 1965.

Mandela, Nelson. *The Struggle is my Life.* London: International Defense and Aid Fund for Southern Africa, 1978.

Mao, Tse-Tung. *Four Essays on Philosophy.* Peking: Foreign Languages Press, 1968.

Marx, Karl, and Engels, Frederick. *The German Ideology.* New York: International Publishers, 1969.

Mbeki, Govan. *South Africa: The Peasants' Revolt.* Baltimore: Penguin Books, 1964.

Moodie, Dunbar T. *The Rise of Afrikanerdom: Power, Apartheid & the Afrikaner Civil Religion.* Berkeley: University of California Press, 1975.

Moore, Barrington. *Injustice: The Social Bases of Obedience and Revolt.* New York: M. E. Sharpe, 1978.

Moore, Basil (ed.). *The Challenge of Black Theology in South Africa.* Atlanta: John Knox Press, 1974.

Murray, Martin J. (ed.). *South African Capitalism and Black Political Opposition.* Cambridge: Schenkman Publishing Company, 1982.

Nengwekhulu, Ranwedzi. *The Meaning of Black Consciousness in the Struggle for Liberation in South Africa.* United Nations, No. 16/76, July 1976.

Nolutshungu, Sam C. *Changing South Africa. Political Considerations.* Manchester: Manchester University Press, 1982.

Rogers, Barbara. *Divide and Rule: South Africa's Bantustans.* London: International Defense and Aid Fund, 1976.

Roux, Edward. *Time Longer Than Rope: A History of the Black Man's Struggle for Freedom in South Africa.* Madison: The University of Wisconsin Press, 1966.

Sassoon, Anne Showstack (ed.). *Approaches to Gramsci.* London: Writers and Readers, 1982.

Saul, John S., and Gelb, Stephen. *The Crisis in South Africa: Class Defense, Class Revolution.* New York: Monthly Review Press, 1981.

Shafer, Boyd C. *Faces of Nationalism.* New York: Harcourt Brace Jovanovich, 1972.

Simons, H. J. and R. E. *Class and Colour in South Africa, 1850–1950.* Middlessex: Penguin Books, 1969.

Sizwe, No. *One Azania, One Nation.* London: Zed Press, 1979.

Smith, Anthony D. *Theories of Nationalism.* New York: Harper Torchbooks, 1971.

Southall, Roger. *South Africa's Transkei.* New York: Monthly Review Press, 1983.

Sundkler, Bengt G. M. *Bantu Prophets in South Africa.* 2nd ed. New York: Oxford University Press, 1961.

Tawney, R. H. *Equality.* New York: Capricorn Books, 1961.

Therborn, Goran. *What Does the Ruling Class Do When It Rules?* London: New Left Review Editions, 1980.

———. *The Ideology of Power and the Power of Ideology.* London: New Editions, 1980.

Thion, Serge. *Le Pouvoir Pâle.* Paris: Editions du Seuil, 1969.

Thompson, E. P. *The Making of the English Working Class.* New York: Vintage Books, 1966.

Thompson, Leonard, and Butler, Jeffrey (ed.). *Change in Contemporary South Africa.* Berkeley: University of California Press, 1975.

———, and Prior, Andrew. *South African Politics.* New Haven: Yale University Press, 1982.

Troup, Freda. *South Africa: An Historical Introduction.* Harmondsworth: Penguin Books, 1975.

Turner, Richard. *The Eye of the Needle.* Johannesburg: A Spro-cas Publication, 1972.

Turok, Ben. *Strategic Problems in South Africa's Liberation Struggle.* Richmond: Liberation Support Movement, 1974.

United Nations, Centre Against Apartheid, Department of Political and Security Council Affairs. *Basic Facts on the Republic of South Africa and the Policy of Apartheid.* New York: 1977.

Van Den Berghe, Pierre L. (ed.). *Africa: Social Problems of Change and Conflict.* San Francisco: Chandler Publishing Company, 1965.

———. *South Africa, A Study in Conflict.* Berkeley: University of California Press, 1967.

Wallerstein, Immanuel. *The Capitalist World-Economy.* Cambridge: University Press, 1979.

Walshe, Peter. *The Rise of African Nationalism in South Africa: The African National Congress, 1912-1952.* Berkeley: University of California Press, 1971.

———. *Black Nationalism in South Africa.* Johannesburg: Ravan Press, 1973.

Wilson, Monica, and Thompson, Leonard (ed.). *The Oxford History of South Africa, Vols. I & II.* New York: Oxford University Press, 1971.

Wolpe, Harold (ed.). *The Articulation of Modes of Production.* London: Routledge & Keegan Paul, 1980.

Woods, Donald. *Biko.* New York: Vintage Books, 1979.

Wright, Harrison M. *The Burden of the Present.* London: David Philip Publishers, 1977.

Zahar, Renate. *Frantz Fanon: Colonialism and Alienation.* New York: Montly Review Press, 1974.

Articles

Adam, Heribert. "The Rise of Black Consciousness in South Africa," *Race,* Volume XV, Number 2 (October 1973), pp. 149–165.

Bartman, E. N. "The Significance of the Development of Black Consciousness for the Church," *SASO Newsletter,* Volume 2, Number 5, pp. 15–18.

Bienefeld, Manfred, and Innes, Duncan. "Capital Accumulation and South Africa," *Review of African Political Economy,* Number 7 (September–December 1976), pp. 31–55.

Birt, Robert E. "An Examination of James Cone's Concept of God and its Role in Black Liberation," *The Philosophical Forum,* Vol. IX, Nox. 2–3 (Winter–Spring 1977–78), pp. 339–349.

"Black Communalism," *Pro Veritate* (June 1976), pp. 6–7.

Blumer, Herbert. "Industrialization and Race Relations," in *Industrialization and Race Relations,* ed. Guy Hunter. London: Oxford University Press, 1965, pp. 220–253.

Boesak, Alan. "Black Consciousness, Black Power and 'Coloured Politics'," *Pro Veritate* (February 1977), pp. 9–12.

Bosch, David. "Currents & Crosscurrents in South African Black Theology," *Journal of Religion in Africa,* VI, 1 (1974), pp. 1–22.

"Briefings," *Review of African Political Economy,* Number 7 (September–December 1976), pp. 108–124.

Buthelezi, Manas. "Black Christians Must Liberate Whites," *Reality,* Vol. 5, No. 3 (July 1973), pp. 3–6.

———. "The Christian Challenge of Black Theology," in *Black Renaissance: Papers from the Black Renaissance Convention,* ed. Thoahlane Thoahlane. Johannesburg: Ravan Press, 1975, pp. 19–23.

"Can Armed Struggle Take Place in Azania?" *Azania News* (June 1977), pp. 2–9.

Carr, Cannon Burgess. "The Black Consciousness Movement in South Africa and Namibia," *Objective: Justice,* Volume 7, Number 3 (July/August/September, 1975), pp. 17–23.

Carter, Gwendolen M. "Black Initiatives for Change in Southern Africa," *Eleventh Melville, Herskovits Memorial Lecture,* Edinburgh University (Friday, 9th March, 1973).

Comaroff, John L. "Chiefship in a South African Homeland," *Journal of Southern African Studies,* Volume 1, Number 1 (October 1974), pp. 36–51.

Cone, James H. "Black Consciousness and the Black Church: An Historical-Theological Interpretation," in *Black Renaissance: Papers from the Black Renaissance Convention,* ed. Thoahlane Thoahlane. Johannesburg: Ravan Press, 1975, pp. 66–72.

Crewe, Adrian. "SASO and Black Consciousness in South Africa," *Reality,* Vol. 3, No. 4 (September 1971), pp. 8–13.

Curtis, Neville, and Keegan, Clive. "The Aspiration to a Just Society," in *Student Perspectives on South Africa.* Ed. Hendrik W. Van der Merwe and David Welsh. Cape Town: David Philip, Publisher, 1972, pp. 95–124.

Davidson, Basil. "Questions about Nationalism," *African Affairs,* Volume 76, Number 302 (January 1977), pp. 39–46.

Davies, Robert. "The White Working-Class in South Africa," *New Left Review,* Number 82 (December 1973), pp. 40–59.

———. "The Class Character of South Africa's Industrial Conciliation Legislation," *South African Labour Bulletin,* Volume 2, Number 6 (January 1976), pp. 6–20.

———. "Mining Capital, The State and Unskilled White Workers in South Africa, 1901–1913," *Journal of Southern African Studies,* Volume 3, Number 1 (October 1976), pp. 41–69.

———, and Lewis, David. "Industrial Relations Legislation: One of Capital's Defenses," *Review of African Political Economy,* Number 7 (September–December 1976), pp. 56–58.

————, Kaplan, David; Morris, Mike; O'Meara, Dan. "Class Struggle and the Periodisation of the State in South Africa," *Review of African Political Economy,* Number 7 (September–December 1976), pp. 4–30.

"Declaration," in *Black Renaissance: Papers from the Black Renaissance Convention,* ed. Thoahlane Thoahlane. Johannesburg: Ravan Press, 1975, pp. 73–75.

"Declaration of Students' Rights," *SASO Newsletter,* Volume 1, Number 3 (August 1971), p. 20.

Fisher, Foszia, and Nxasana, Harold. "The Labour Situation in South Africa," *South African Labour Bulletin,* Volume 2, Number 2 (July 1975), pp. 43–51.

Frankel, Philip. "Black Power in South Africa," *New Nation,* Vol. 6, No. 3 (October 1972), pp. 3–7.

Franklin, Raymond S. "The Political Economy of Black Power," *Social Problems,* Vol. 16, No. 3 (Winter 1969), pp. 286–301.

Gann, Lewis. "No Hope for Violent Liberation: A Strategic Assessment," *Africa Report* (1972), pp. 15–19.

Gerwel, C. J. "Black Power: S. A.," *South African Outlook,* Vol. 103, Number 1226 (July 1973), pp. 119–120.

Gewel, G. J. "The Blackman—His Compassion," *SASO Newsletter,* Volume 2, Number 5 (November/December 1972), pp. 8–9.

Glass, Humphrey. "The Struggle for South Africa," *Monthly Review,* Volume 28, Number 7 (December 1976), pp. 7–24.

Greenberg, Stanley B. "Economic Growth and Political Change: The South African Case," *The Journal of Modern African Studies,* Vol. 19, Number 4 (1981), pp. 667–704.

Gwala, Pascal M. "The Black Thing . . . is Honest . . . is Human," *SASO Newsletter,* Volume 2, Number 1 (January/February 1972), pp. 13–15.

————. "Towards the Practical Manifestations of Black Consciousness," in *Black Renaissance: Papers from the Black Renaissance Convention.* Ed. Thoahlane Thoahlane. Johannesburg: Ravan Press, 1975, pp. 24–33.

Innes, Duncan, and O'Meara, Dan. "Class Formation and Ideology: The Transkei Region," *Review of African Political Economy,* Number 7 (September–December 1976), pp. 69–86.

Johns, Sheridan. "Obstacles of Guerrilla Warfare—A South African Case Study," *The Journal of Modern African Studies,* Volume 11, Number 2 (1973), pp. 124–140.

Johnstone, Frederick A. "White Prosperity and White Supremacy in South Africa Today," *African Affairs,* Volume 69, Number 275 (April 1970), pp. 124–140.

————. "The Ongoing Debate over the Neo-Marxist Analysis of South Africa: The Poverty of Kantor-Kenny Case," Paper presented at the *7th Conference of the Canadian Association of African Studies,* University of Sherbrooke (3–6 May, 1977).

Kantor, B. S., and Kenny, H. F. "The Poverty of Neo-Marxism: The Case of South Africa," *Journal of Southern African Studies,* Volume 3, Number 1 (October 1976), pp. 20–40.

Khoapa, Bennie A. "The New Black," in *Black Viewpoint,* ed. Steve Biko. Durban: SPRO-CAS, 1972, pp. 61–67.

Langa, Bhekie. "Black Consciousness and the Black Community," *SASO Newsletter,* Volume 5, Number 1 (May/June 1975), pp. 9–12.

Legassick, Martin. "The Frontier Tradition in South African Historiography," *Collected Seminar Papers on the Societies of Southern Africa in the 19th and 20th Centuries,* University of London Institute of Commonwealth Studies, Volume 2, Number 12 (October 1970–June 1971), pp. 1–33.

————. "The Dynamics of Modernization in South Africa," *Journal of African History,* Volume XIII, Number 1 (1972), pp. 145–150.

————. "South Africa: Capital Accumulation and Violence," *Economy and Society,* Volume 3, Number 3 (August 1974), pp. 253–291.

————. "Legislation, Ideology and Economy in Post 1948 South Africa," *Journal of Southern African Studies,* Volume 1, Number 1 (October 1974), pp. 5–35.

————. "The Record of British Firms in South Africa: In the Context of the Political Economy," *South African Labour Bulletin,* Volume 2, Number 1 (May–June 1975), pp. 7–36.

————. "Race, Industrialization and Social Change in South Africa: The Case of R. F. A. Hoernle," *African Affairs,* Volume 75, Number 299 (April 1976), pp. 224–239.

————. "Records of Protest and Challenge," *Journal of African History,* 20, 3 (1979), pp. 451–455.

————, and Wolpe, Harold. "The Bantustans and Capital Accumulation in South Africa," *Review of African Political Economy,* Number 7 (September–December 1976), pp. 87–107.

————, and Innes, Duncan. "Capital Restructuring and Apartheid: A Critique of Constructive Engagement," *African Affairs,* Volume 76, Number 305 (October 1977), pp. 437–482.

Lipton, Merle. "The Debate About South Africa: Neo-Marxists and Neo-Liberals," *African Affairs,* Volume 78, Number 310 (January 1979), pp. 57–80.

Mafeje, Archie. "Religion, Class and Ideology in South Africa," in *Religion and Social Change in Southern Africa,* ed. Michael G. Whisson and Martin West. Cape Town: 1975, pp. 164–184.

————. "Soweto and its Aftermath," *Review of African Political Economy.* 11 (1978), pp. 17–30. Reprinted in Martin J. Murray (ed.) *South African Capitalism and Black Political Opposition.* Cambridge: Schenkman, 1982, pp. 739–759.

Mafungo, Vic. "Black Theology," *SASO Newsletter,* Volume 1, Number 4 (September 1971), pp. 7–9.

Magagula, S. T. M. "Black Power," (1973).

Magubane, Ben. "African Opposition in South Africa," *The African Review,* Volume 2, Number 3, (1972), pp. 433–447.

Mandela, Winnie. "We Shall Establish a Socialist Republic of Azania," *Azania Combat* (January–April 1977), p. 1.

Marks, Shula. "Liberalism, Social Realities, and South African History," *Journal of Commonwealth Political Studies,* Volume X, Number 3 (November 1972), pp. 243–249.

Marquard, Leo. "Black Consciousness," *Reality,* Vol. 5, No. 4 (September 1973), p. 10.

Mason, David. "Industrialisation, Race and Class Conflict in South Africa: Towards a Sociological Restoration of a Reopened Debate," *Ethnic and Racial Studies,* 3, 2 (April 1980), pp. 140–155.

Meer, Fatima. "The Black Woman in South Africa," in *Black Renaissance: Papers from the Black Renaissance Convention,* ed. Thoahlane Thoahlane. Johannesburg: Ravan Press, 1975, pp. 34–46.

Mkhatshwa, S. P. "Introduction," in *Black Renaissance: Papers from the Black Renaissance Convention,* ed. Thoahlane Thoahlane. Johannesburg: Ravan Press, 1975, pp. 10–12.

Molteno, Frank. "The Uprising of 16th June: A Review of the Literature on Events in South Africa 1976," *Social Dynamics,* 5, 1 (1979), pp. 18–20.

Mothopeng, Z. "Imperialist Penetration into African Universities," *SASO Newsletter,* Volume 5, Number 2 (July/August 1975), pp. 4–5.

Motsuenyane, S. M. "Black Consciousness and the Economic Position of the Black Man in South Africa," in *Black Renaissance: Papers from the Black Renaissance Convention,* ed. Thoahlane Thoahlane. Johannesburg: Ravan Press, 1975, pp. 47–52.

Mugomba, Agrippah. "Liberation Ecumenicalism and Armed Struggle in Southern Africa," Paper presented at the *Annual Convention of the African Studies Association,* Houston, 2–5 November 1977.

Murphy, Mike. "What the Black Workers Think," *Reality,* Vol. 4, No. 5 (November 1972), pp. 4–6.

Naidoo, Dilly. "The Role of Black Organizations in the Life of the Community," *SASO Newsletter,* Volume 2, Number 1 (January/February 1972), pp. 18–20.

Nairn, Tom. "The Modern Janus," *New Left Review,* Number 94 (November–December 1975), pp. 3–29.

Ndebele, Njabulo. "Black Development," in *Black Viewpoint,* ed. Steve Biko. Durban: SPRO-CAS, 1972, pp. 13–28.

Nengwekhulu, Ranwedzi. "Black Consciousness Movement of South Africa," Paper read at the *Assembly of the I.U.E.F.,* Geneva (November 23, 1976).

Nettleton, Clive. "Racial Cleavage on the Student Left," in *Student Perspectives on South Africa.* Ed. Hendrik W. Van der Merwe and David Welsh. Cape Town: David Philip Publisher, 1972, pp. 125–137.

Nkondo, Gessler Moses. "The Educational World of Blacks in South Africa," in *Black Renaissance: Papers from the Black Renaissance Convention,* ed. Thoahlane Thoahlane. Johannesburg: Ravan Press, 1975, pp. 13–18.

O'Meara, Dan. "White Trade Unionism, Political Power and Afrikaner Nationalism," *South African Labour Bulletin,* Volume 1, Number 10 (April 1975), pp. 31–51.

———. "The 1946 African Mine Workers' Strike and the Political Economy of South Africa," *The Journal of Commonwealth & Comparative Politics,* Volume XIII, Number 2 (July 1975), pp. 146–173.

———. "The Afrikaner Broederbond 1927–1948: Class Vanguard of Afrikaner Nationalism," *Journal of Southern African Studies,* Volume 3, Number 2 (April 1977), pp. 156–186.

———. "Analyzing Afrikaner Nationalism: The 'Christian National' Assault on White Trade Unionism in South Africa, 1934–1948," *African Affairs,* Volume 77, Number 306 (January 1978), pp. 45–72.

Petryszak, Nicholas. "The Dynamics of Acquiescence in South Africa," *African Affairs,* Volume 75, Number 301 (October 1976), pp. 444–462.

Pityana, Barney. "Re: South African Students' Organization (SASO)," no date.

———. "The 2nd General Students Council, An Assessment," *SASO Newsletter,* Volume 1, Number 3 (August 1971), pp. 3–4.

———. "Priorities in Community Development—An Appeal to the Blackman's Compassion," *SASO Newsletter,* Volume 1, Number 4 (September 1971), pp. 13–16.

———. "Re: SASO v. NIC Controversy," SASO: March 1972.

———. "Power and Social Change in South Africa," in *Student Perspectives on South Africa,* ed. Hendrik W. Van der Merwe and David Welsh. Cape Town: David Philip Publisher, 1972, pp. 174–189.

Randall, Peter. "Only Socialism Can Satisfy South Africa's Future," *Pro Veritate* (March 1977), pp. 8–10.

Rathbone, Richard. "Students and Politics: South Africa," *The Journal of Commonwealth & Comparative Politics,* Volume XV, Number 2 (July 1977), pp. 105–111.

Rebusoajoang. "Educational and Social Control in South Africa," *African Affairs,* Vol. 78, Number 311 (April 1979), pp. 228–239.

"SASO Manifesto," *SASO Newsletter,* Volume 1, Number 3 (August 1971), pp. 10–11.

"SASO Opinion," *SASO Newsletter,* Volume 1, Number 4 (September 1971), pp. 4–6.

Shepherd, George W. Jr. "Liberation Theology and Class Struggle in Southern Africa and Latin America," *The Review of Black Political Economy,* Vol. 9, No. 2 (Winter 1979), pp. 159–173.

Smiley, Xan. "South Africa: What is Black?" *The New York Review of Books,* Volume XXVI, Number 6 (April 19, 1979), pp. 22–28.

Sono, Temba. "An Interview with our President Temba 'Joe' Sono," *SASO Newsletter,* Volume 1, Number 3 (August 1971), pp. 8–9.

———. "Solitaire, Solitariness and Solidarity," *SASO Newsletter,* Volume 2, Number 1 (January/February 1972), pp. 5–7.

———. "In Search of a Free & New Society," (July 1972).

Southall, Roger J. "The Beneficiaries of Transkeian 'Independence'," *The Journal of Modern African Studies,* Volume 15, Number 1 (1977), pp. 1–23.

"The 3rd General Students' Council—An Assessment," *SASO Newsletter,* Volume 2, Number 4 (September/October 1972), pp. 13–15.

"The Transkei Independence," *SASO Newsletter,* Volume 6, Number 1 (March/April 1976), pp. 1–2.

Thoahlane, Thoahlane. "Foreword," in *Black Renaissance: Papers from the Black Renaissance Convention,* ed. Thoahlane Thoahlane. Johannesburg: Ravan Press, 1975, pp. 7–9.

Trapido, Stanley. "South Africa in a Comparative Study of Industrialization," *The Journal of Development Studies,* Volume 7, Number 3 (April 1971), pp. 309–320.

———. "South Africa and the Historians," *African Affairs,* Volume 71, Number 285 (October 1972), pp. 444–448.

Turner, Richard. "Black Consciousness and White Liberals," *Reality* (July 1972), pp. 20–22.

Turok, Ben. "South Africa: The Violent Alternative," in *The Socialist Register 1972,* ed. Ralph Miliband and John Saville. London: The Merlin Press, 1972, pp. 257–288.

Turok, Ben. "South Africa: The Search for a Strategy," in *The Socialist Register 1973,* ed. Ralph Miliband and John Saville. London: The Merlin Press, 1974, pp. 341–376.

Walshe, Peter. "Church versus State in South Africa: The Christian Institute and the Resurgence of African Nationalism," *Journal of Church and State,* Volume 19, Number 3 (Autumn 1977), pp. 457–479.

Watcher, Scene. "Change and the Man at the Top," *SASO Newsletter,* Volume 5, Number 2 (July/August 1975), pp. 10–12.

Williams, Gwyn. "The Concept of 'Egemonia' in the Thought of Antonio Gramsci: Some Notes on Interpretation," *Journal of the History of Ideas,* Vol. XXI, No. 4 (October/December 1960), pp. 586–599.

Wolpe, Harold. "Industrialism and Race in South Africa," in *Race and Racialism,* ed. Sami Zubaida. London: Tavistock Publications, 1970, pp. 151–179.

———. "Class, Race and the Occupational Structure," *Collected Seminar Papers on the Societies of Southern Africa in the 19th and 20th Centuries,* University of London, Institute of Commonwealth Studies, Volume 2, Number 12 (October 1970–June 1971), pp. 98–119.

Wolpe, Harold. "Capitalism and Cheap Labour-Power in South Africa: From Segregation to Apartheid," *Economy and Society,* Volume 1, Number 4 (November 1972), pp. 425–456.

———. "The Theory of Internal Colonialism: The South African Case," in *Beyond the Sociology of Development,* ed. Ivar Oxaal,

Tony Barnet and David Booth. London and Boston: Routledge & Keegan Paul, 1975, pp. 229–252.

——. "The 'White Working Class' in South Africa," *Economy and Society,* Volume 5, Number 2 (May 1976), pp. 197–240.

Yudelman, David. "Industrialization, Race Relations and Change in South Africa: An Ideological and Academic Debate," *African Affairs,* Vol. 74, Number 194 (January 1975), pp. 82–96.

Zani, Tami. "The Future Society as Seen by Black People's Convention," *Pro Veritate* (June 1977), pp. 11–12.

Zwane, Madlenkosi A. "Social Communications (Mass Media) Among a Developing People," in *Black Renaissance: Papers from the Black Renaissance Convention,* ed. Thoahlane Thoahlane. Johannesburg: Ravan Press, 1975, pp. 59–65.

Periodicals Consulted

African Communist.
Ikwezi.
Pro Veritate.
Reality.
SASO Newsletter.
Sechaba.
The Star, International Airmail Weekly.

INDEX

187

DATE DUE

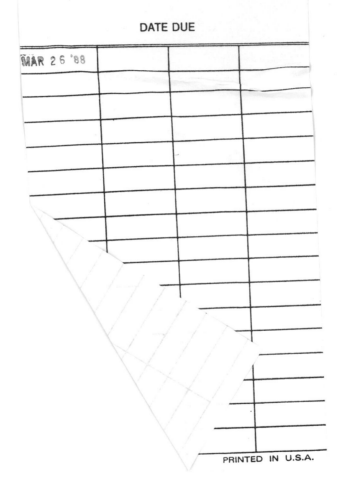

MAR 26 '88

PRINTED IN U.S.A.